W9-BOO-708

NEW KITCHEN
IDEAS THAT WORK

NEW KITCHEN IDEAS THAT WORK

JAMIE GOLD

The Taunton Press

Dedication

To my mother—my first, best, and most-missed role model—whose insights inspire me still, and to Megan, with whom I love sharing her wisdom.

Text © 2012 by The Taunton Press, Inc.
Illustrations © 2012 by The Taunton Press, Inc.
All rights reserved.

The Taunton Press
Inspiration for hands-on living®

The Taunton Press, Inc.
63 South Main Street, PO Box 5506
Newtown, CT 06470-5506
e-mail: tp@taunton.com

Editor: Carolyn Mandarano
Copy editor: Seth Reichgott
Indexer: Jay Kreider
Interior design: Carol Petro
Layout: David Giammattei
Illustrator: Christine Erikson
Cover photographers: Front cover (top, left to right): © Ryann Ford; (large): © Eric Roth; back cover (top left) © Susan Teare; (top center): © Susan Teare; (top right): © Mark Lohman; (center): Formica Corporation; (bottom left): © Mark Lohman; (bottom right): © Greg Riegler

Library of Congress Cataloging-in-Publication Data

Gold, Jamie, 1960-
  New kitchen ideas that work / Jamie Gold.
      pages cm
  Includes index.
  ISBN 978-1-60085-496-5
1. Kitchens–Remodeling. 2. Interior decoration. I. Title.
  TH4816.3.K58G65 2012
  690'.44–dc23

                           2012029385

Printed in the United States of America
10 9 8 7

The following names/manufacturers appearing in *New Kitchen Ideas That Work* are trademarks: Advantage™ Trim and Lumber; Archadeck®; AstroTURF®; Backyard America™; Cambria®, Cambrian Black™, Chief Architect®; Deckorators®; Feeney® Architectural Products; IKEA®, InSinkErator®, Kalamazoo™ Outdoor Gourmet; Kensington™, KitchenAid®, Sketchup™; Staron®, Total 3D™; Trex®.

ACKNOWLEDGMENTS

Writing this book has been a phenomenal experience and I'm so grateful to so many people for their tireless support and guidance in its creation.

I am thankful for my colleagues at The Taunton Press, including Erin Giunta, Katy Binder, Sharon Zagata, Deb Silber, Peter Chapman, Seth Reichgott, Christine Erikson, Janel Noblin, and my editor, Carolyn Mandarano, who gave me the opportunity to write a book for a publisher I have long respected and who expertly guided me through the process.

This book would be much shorter and less beautiful without the talented designers who contributed their kitchen projects for the case studies: Jeff Krieger, Tiffany Rose Leichter, Tom McElroy, Lisa Wilson-Wirth, Tom Richard, Ines Hanl, Cheryl Nagle Kees Clendenon, Tara Anderson, Karen Thompson, Kelly Morisseau, Susan Serra, and Terry Smith (with whom I collaborated on Chapter 2's Compact, Contemporary Family Kitchen sidebar). In addition to the designers, I am grateful to their tireless representatives and to the photographers whose talents did justice to their designs and who provided other images.

I would like to additionally thank the following colleagues who generously shared their specialized knowledge with me: Dean Larkin, Arne Salvesen, Terry Smith, Debbie Schaeffer, the Warner family (Julie, Jeff, and Angela), David VanWert, Diane Williams, Ryan Fasan, Darius Helm, Jenny Maedgen, Bob Borson, Gus Morgutia, Sheen Fischer, Molly McLane, Dan Sullivan, Amy Gil, and Vicky Lodge.

On the personal side, I'd like to thank my wonderful family for their unwavering love and support, especially my father. I couldn't have asked for better roots--or wings. I'd also like to thank those friends who have been like a second family for me in all the best ways possible. I love each and every one of you.

Finally, my authorship of this book would not have been possible without my professional friends in the architecture, construction, and design worlds, all of whom have shared their time and knowledge with me so generously over the years. I particularly thank Brian Guerard for taking a chance on hiring someone with no related experience for my first kitchen design job all those years ago. I'm thrilled that this book will end up on your racks, the same ones I walked past every day in those earliest years of my kitchen and bath career.

CONTENTS

CHAPTER 8

Decorative Touches 184

INTRODUCTION

Some of my favorite childhood memories take me back to our family kitchen. I can see my father improvising a rich chocolate mousse for my Sweet 16 party. And when I listen to "Crocodile Rock" and "Honky Tonk Woman" as I work at my desk, I'm taken back to youthful evenings cleaning up after dinner with my mother and sister, bopping along to those very same songs.

So much of our life happens in the kitchen—the ones we grew up in and the ones we own today. Graduations are preceded by hundreds of math problems worked out on a chair, a stool, a countertop, a table. A lifetime of holiday meals are prepared in crowded ovens and cast iron skillets, while extended families catch up on the seasons between celebrations.

The changes in our kitchens through the decades have been designed to enhance these gatherings and simplify our daily chores. New layout ideas take down the walls between cook and guests and reduce steps between task and completion. New technologies make preparing meals and cleaning up afterward easier, more eco-friendly, and, thankfully, faster. (My stepdaughter doesn't have to roll the dishwasher to the sink and hook its hose to the faucet to run it as I did growing up!) New products provide greater durability, safety, and eco-friendly benefits.

Every chapter features a New Vision sidebar, which provides information and photographs on some of the smartest, most useful advances in the kitchen industry in recent years--think appliances that do the work of two or three in the space of one and lights that last for 10 to 20 years and cut your electric bills. In these pages, you'll find both new approaches to planning your space and new resources for equipping it.

Not everything in your new kitchen needs to be new either. So many remodels preserve existing elements like flooring and appliances or phase in new ones over time, as need and budgets dictate. For projects like these, I've included a section in each chapter called Working with What You Have. These sidebars are designed to help you update your kitchen in a way that makes sense for both that space as well as the surrounding rooms.

Enhancing your kitchen is an investment in your home, and this book is designed to make that investment as smart and stylish as possible. So before you plan an entirely new—or newly improved—kitchen, read this book to help guide your choices for your home and your family, so that your investment of time and money will be worth it in the end.

TURNING

Your new kitchen will add style and convenience

to your life and value to your home.

YOUR DREAM

First you must make some important decisions

before investing your hard-earned money.

INTO REALITY

Assess Your Needs

If you've decided to remodel your kitchen—or even if you're still just thinking about it—the question you're likely to ask yourself is where to start. It's best to begin the process by assessing your needs. Chances are you've already started doing this without even realizing it. You've probably taken stock of irritants like chipped countertop edges and peeling doors. You've noted not only how much you've hated the cabinets since you bought the house, but also how much you wish for more light. These and other points like them are excellent to include in your assessment, but they aren't necessarily the starting point.

An assessment should be based on how you and your family will really use the new kitchen on a daily basis. Begin your assessment with what already works well in and around the kitchen and which elements you want to keep. These become the starting points for the remodel and help determine the scope of work. For example, if the tile that runs into the kitchen and covers most of the main floor is in good shape and a style you like, you may want to keep it. What this means, though, is that you'll be keeping the kitchen's footprint pretty much the same, especially if the flooring is hard to match or replace, and you'll be choosing cabinetry and countertops that coordinate with it. These are important notes for your assessment.

Monochromatic white and pale gray finishes make this compact kitchen appear larger. The peninsula shelves and minimalist window treatments enhance the feeling of openness.

above · The stone tops, blonde floors, and colorful rug warm up this transitional kitchen equipped with pro-style stainless appliances.

above · This kitchen takes great advantage of abundant natural light with a window seat for dining and gray finishes that keep the space visually cool.

If you've recently purchased a home, go ahead and create an assessment, but use your kitchen for at least three months before starting a remodeling process. That will really highlight its strengths and weaknesses and allow you to focus your resources where they'll do the most good. What may have been an original wish list item may no longer fit your priorities when you start remodeling months later.

Include storage, counter space, artificial lighting and natural light, layout, flooring, appliances, and fixtures in your assessment. What works and what doesn't? What changes are essential or just desirable? (The latter may give way to other priorities in the planning process.) What new or future needs, like an older parent moving in, new children in the household, or your own aging process, should be factored into the remodel?

Assessing your needs in this detailed, analytic manner will help you get the best kitchen possible as well as the best return on your remodeling investment.

top right • A full kitchen assessment should address clutter. This clever corner organizes mail, books, and phone in colorful style, then hides clutter behind a pocket door when not in use.

right • Light from the exterior door glass, sink window, and tubular skylight are strong elements in this kitchen. Renovations to a space that has these features should take advantage of them.

Start a kitchen assessment with those elements worth keeping. In this cheerful kitchen, the framed arch window, handsome wood floors, and folk art collection are all potential starting points for inspiration and coordination.

Facelift or Full Remodel

Sometimes a kitchen doesn't need a full remodel, just a facelift. (Sometimes that's all your budget will allow, as well.) Your needs assessment will help you determine which option is right for you and your home. If your current cabinets are structurally sound and you're keeping your existing footprint to preserve the flooring, you could be an excellent candidate for cabinet refacing or refinishing. Neither of these cosmetic improvements will add storage to your kitchen, but both could give it a new look. A cabinet facelift can also include the addition of storage accessories, decorative molding, and new hardware.

Another kind of facelift could bypass your cabinetry entirely, one that involves replacing or resurfacing the countertops on top of the existing base cabinets. Most often, this change will be from laminate to natural or engineered stone. One note, though: This generally entails changing the faucet, sink, and drains, as well. These upgrades offer you the opportunity to improve functionality while you're improving your kitchen's style. For example, you can choose a sink with a better bowl configuration and upgrade to a pull-out faucet with a coordinating soap dispenser for greater convenience.

Updating the lighting is another form of kitchen facelift. You can change out old-style fluorescent light boxes in favor of recessed can lights without making any other changes in the space. Or install pendants over islands and peninsulas for a better-lit, better-looking space. You can also convert recessed lights to pendants, if you prefer that look, and add undercabinet lighting to improve your work areas. Of course, a licensed electrician is the best person to make these changes.

A change in flooring also can enhance a kitchen's functionality as well as its style. New flooring can be more comfortable cork, for instance, or more durable porcelain. Whatever choice you make, it is crucial to consider the new material's specifications so that you avoid unexpected consequences, like locking a dishwasher into place.

above · A lowered counter provides a convenient spot for children, wheelchair users, or seniors to share kitchen chores or meals with the household.

right · A vivid blue glass backsplash, open wall cabinets, and sleek brushed hardware can freshen up an existing kitchen without a major investment.

Countertop Resurfacing

In recent years, new systems have been developed that allow for installing a stone top directly over existing counters. These countertop systems are most often made from a thin layer of engineered stone to achieve the new look and performance rather than from the standard 2cm or 3cm slab of stone. Concrete and porcelain resurfacing are also available, but not in all areas of the country.

The chief benefit of these countertop resurfacing systems is reduced demolition and kitchen downtime. The limitations include a narrow range of styles to choose from, relatively high cost, and a limited number of companies performing them. You can research this in your area by looking up "countertop resurfacing" on the Internet, but be sure to check references, licensing, and work performed for others in your local area.

A SWOT Analysis for Your Kitchen

A SWOT analysis (identifying strengths, weaknesses, opportunities, and threats) is a common business practice that was put to good use for the owners of a hundred-year-old Philadelphia Colonial. They loved the home's stonework and slate roof, but the chopped-up floor plan, so typical of its era, was disrupting the flow of the home. They especially knew the dated, disjointed kitchen had to be improved.

With the help of a local architect, the homeowners created the following SWOT analysis for their kitchen renovation.

- **Strengths:** Good location near rear door and adjacent to laundry/family/breakfast rooms; window to rear yard.

- **Weaknesses:** Poor layout of appliances; inadequate upper cabinet storage; no visual connection to family room; outdated finishes; poor lighting.

- **Opportunities:** Open up the kitchen to the family room for better interaction and to the patio for outdoor dining; provide better cooking surfaces; add seating at the island; update finishes; improve and increase storage.

- **Threats:** Dangerously inadequate ventilation: 48-inch Viking® range uses hood from previous 30-inch range.

The plan the homeowners and architect created as a result of this detailed analysis successfully addressed these areas and updated the kitchen so that it fit the old home's character and the homeowners' modern lifestyle.

above • Wine cubbies take stylish advantage of otherwise wasted space near the ceiling; a step ladder to reach them for occasional entertaining can be tucked away in the nearby laundry room.

left • One of the original kitchen's weaknesses was inadequate cooking ventilation. A new properly sized vent hood pulls cooking grease and gases out of the handsome new room and removes a former hazard.

right • Painted Shaker-style cabinets, oak floor, and granite countertops tie into the home's traditional architecture. New appliances, clever storage, and sleek finishes update it for modern living.

above • A good location was one of the original kitchen's strengths. The new design took advantage of this location by opening the room to the adjacent family room and patio for better living flow.

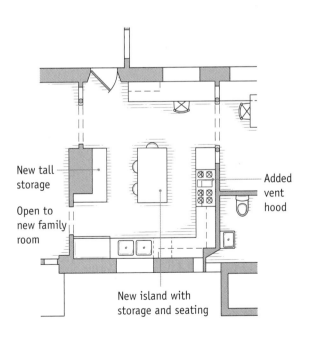

New tall storage

Open to new family room

Added vent hood

New island with storage and seating

The Big Picture

Whether you're planning a facelift or a full-scale remodel, it's essential to factor in the major elements staying in the kitchen or adjacent rooms that open to the kitchen. These include architecture, flooring, and built-ins. What you change in the space should coordinate with what you're keeping.

For example, consider the size and style of moldings, built-ins, or a fireplace surround that will stay, and incorporate that detail into the new kitchen design. Choose cabinetry finishes and countertops that work not just with the kitchen flooring (new or existing), but with the flooring and built-ins in rooms that open onto the kitchen.

Generally, you don't need to take furniture into account when selecting permanent elements, but there is a notable exception. If you have a large, valuable focal-point piece, like an antique library cabinet or oversize heirloom hutch, you may want to coordinate with it, as well, by selecting complementary styles and finishes for the updated kitchen. Smaller furniture, paint, cabinet knobs, and similar small items don't need to factor into your plans, as they're relatively easy and inexpensive to change later, if you wish.

Replace the country sheers for a better-coordinated faux wood blind more in keeping with the room's style. Colored tapes tie into the new cabinet finish.

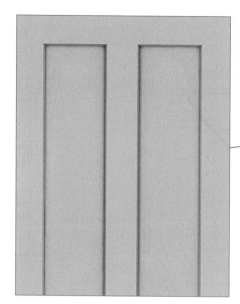

If the wood backsplash, wood floors, wood walls, and wood beams give you cabin fever, the cabinets can be refaced or refinished in a mid-toned historic-inspired paint.

THE EXISTING ROOM

A smart kitchen update should work with, not against, the architecture of the space. New additions and replacements for this room should coordinate with the existing Craftsman architecture.

Family-friendly quartz countertops can take an integral sink, but are stain-resistant and require no sealing like the natural slate ones currently installed. A full-height backsplash in the same material would also simplify clean-up and add updated style to this kitchen.

Consider Styles

Determining your kitchen's style has as much to do with the elements in that room as your home's architecture, particularly if your kitchen opens up to rooms around it. No less important is the consideration of your lifestyle and personal tastes.

The three main style groups from which you'll choose include traditional, transitional, and modern. (The term contemporary is often used interchangeably with modern.)

TRADITIONAL

Traditional kitchens often incorporate detailed moldings and door styles; painted, distressed, glazed, or stained cabinetry; decorative countertop edges; and old-world-inspired faucets and light fixtures. They look most at home in traditional houses. However, consider the extra time involved in dusting decorative carvings and applied door moldings if you're the primary house cleaner. Perhaps a simple, transitional style will work for you instead.

TRANSITIONAL

Transitional kitchens are inspired by traditional designs but offer cleaner, pared-down lines. Recessed door styles, simple moldings, and eased countertop edges characterize the transitional kitchen. In most cases, they'll coordinate with a traditional or modern house. They're especially well suited to Craftsman-style architecture.

left • Decorative legs, beadboard detailing on some of the island doors, oak floors, and a bridge faucet all reinforce the country credentials of this traditional kitchen.

below • Subtle details like the Shaker arch on the hood, simple top molding, and bronze cabinet hardware enhance the Craftsman style of this kitchen.

The transitional details in this kitchen, like its bin pull hardware and inset cabinet doors, complement the room's traditional architecture without adding visual clutter.

MODERN

Modern kitchens strive for a no-fuss look with slab door styles, integral or sleek hardware, no moldings, wood grain or high-gloss finishes, and countertops with minimal detail. Modern kitchens fit most comfortably in a modern home but are increasingly found in traditional homes, as well.

If your household includes active children or pets, consider whether finger and paw prints that show easily on glossy surfaces will be an issue for you. Perhaps a wood-grain slab door or easy-to-clean tile floor will be the best fit for your household.

ECLECTIC

Eclectic kitchens are creative but uncommon and typically blend elements from two or more styles. Most often you'll see this when a unique piece of furniture, an appliance, or a lighting element is combined with cabinetry of another style.

left • Slab doors, minimalist hardware, pared-down chandelier, and zero molding proclaim this kitchen's modern style. Natural elements, like the cabinets' strong wood grain and the forested view, provide the room's decorative detail.

above • The stained-glass window and vintage range coexist stylishly with the modern hood and restaurant-style faucet in this very eclectic kitchen.

Collecting Ideas

There has never been a better time to find inspiration for your kitchen project. Beyond the books, magazines, home tours, and home shows, there are now websites, blogs, social media pages, smartphone apps, and online magazines to assist your search as well.

Inspiration is great, but what works for a 7,000-square-foot mansion in Malibu may not work for your compact condo in Kansas City. Any plans to create or update a kitchen should include insights from your own area. That way, what you plan for your home will be in keeping with neighborhood standards and local architecture, including, of course, your own. Too often, buyer's remorse comes from a fabulous new kitchen not working with the older dining room and great room.

Check out projects in your area by visiting model homes or viewing real estate listings online. Review them with a critical eye. Are the refrigerators built-in or freestanding? Are the countertops stone or Corian®? Does the kitchen feature contemporary or traditional cabinets? Are the floors wood or tile? These all point to what's valued in your area and can help inform your project.

Improvise in your own style, too. While assimilating the wisdom of your market and the architecture of your home as guiding principles, you also want to incorporate your own taste in crafting the kitchen of your dreams.

The key is to stay focused and organized. The ideas you collect will help your professional team create the kitchen you envision, tailored to your home, needs, and budget.

Whether you look for ideas in books, online, or at local events, be sure the elements that inspire you will not only work well with your home's architecture and value, but also with how you use your kitchen.

"Greening" Your Kitchen

"Green" kitchens have been growing in popularity in recent years as homeowners make material choices that affect their homes, families, and the world around them. How you define "green" speaks to your personal values, and it's important to make your professional team aware of your concerns and desires before hiring them. These choices can affect systems, as well as the kitchen footprint, and be more expensive than standard options.

For some, a greener kitchen is one that has a lower impact on the planet. For many of these eco-conscious individuals, reusing or donating existing items in the home, sourcing new materials within 500 miles of the project site to minimize the project's carbon footprint, ensuring that the items specified are from responsibly managed sources, and building in recycling and composting centers are important to achieving a green kitchen.

Others look for water-saving faucets and energy-saving appliances and lighting to not only make their kitchens greener but also save money on their utility bills. Other green and money-saving projects could include window replacement to allow in more natural light and increase utility savings.

For others—especially those with health concerns—a greener kitchen is one that uses materials that won't impact their immune systems. For remodels that keep this concern in mind, select cabinetry, flooring, construction adhesives, and paint that won't release chemicals into the home, sometimes called "off-gassing." More options for homeowners that go this route include incorporating water filtration and the best possible cooking ventilation as an added precaution against pollutants.

A kitchen that's eco-friendly can also be style-friendly. Energy-efficient lighting and water-saving appliances, as well as the abundance of natural light, contribute to this kitchen's green credentials. So do cabinets made from responsibly harvested trees that don't contain health-damaging materials or finishes.

above • The bar top in this kitchen is not just a design focal point. It's also an eco-friendly surface made from recycled glass bottles.

Greenwashing

The growing popularity of environmentally friendly products has bred some misleading messages in the marketplace. This practice of "greenwashing" by some manufacturers and contractors is intended to steer you toward product selections that may be no better than their less-expensive counterparts. Be a skeptic. Ask about specific benefits in one brand claim versus another to be sure your priorities are being met. Don't assume that all labels and certifications have equal value. New ones that lack proven science arrive on the scene regularly. The advent of the Internet gives you and your designer the power to research product claims and dubious certifications. Because your health, values, and budget are all at stake, do your homework or choose a professional who already has.

An Aging-in-Place Kitchen

Most of us want to remain in our homes after we retire, but only a fraction of the nation's housing stock is built with aging or accessibility in mind. Although this is slowly changing, incorporating aging-in-place features into your kitchen is a good investment in your future needs, regardless of your age today. It may also improve your kitchen remodel's return on investment if you do sell your home.

AGING-IN-PLACE ELEMENTS

With homeowners staying in place longer and welcoming in older family members who might have physical limitations, it's essential to remodel your kitchen for long-term living. Although the list below includes elements to consider for those with particular physical impairments, many of these suggestions benefit all family members, disabled or not.

- **Accessible seating:** As balance becomes more challenging with age and increased fatigue calls for seated food preparation, replace bar stools and high bars with counter stools, chairs, and tables.

- **Ample lighting:** Incorporate task lighting to illuminate all work surfaces, use interior lights to illuminate large storage areas, and provide ambient room lights to make dining, reading, and conversation areas comfortable for the reduced vision that often accompanies aging.

- **Comfortable, slip-resistant flooring:** Standing on hard surfaces for long periods is stressful to older joints and bones, and falls are one of the leading dangers for older adults. With this in mind, use cork, linoleum, wood, or cushioned mats instead of hard, slick floors. Anti-slip treatments can help those who crave stone flooring despite its drawbacks.

- **Quiet, effective ventilation:** Many homeowners don't use a range hood because it's noisy and inefficient. This can lead both to pollutants irritating fragile respiratory systems and to increased difficulty communicating because of hearing issues. A hood with a countertop-installed remote control can be easier to operate for someone with osteoporosis.

Good cooking ventilation is essential for healthy aging. A remote control installed in the countertop makes it easy to use for someone with balance issues, mobility challenges, or osteoporosis.

- **Accessible cabinet hardware and faucets:** Gripping knobs is more challenging for older hands, so plan handles, wide finger-pull spaces, touch latches, or motion openers for cabinetry and lever handles or touch and sensor systems for faucets.

- **Cabinet accessories:** Roll-out trays, lazy Susans, swing-out storage, and pull-down shelves make accessing cabinet interiors easier on the back for less-flexible adults.

- **Smart appliance planning:** Refrigerator and dishwasher drawers can help create kitchen zones that reduce steps and fatigue. Wall ovens and microwaves mounted at comfortable heights are easier to reach inside than the oven on a range. Side-opening ovens are easier for wheelchair users to operate.

- **Multiple countertop heights:** Table-height workspaces are ideal for seated kitchen tasks. This can be achieved with supported overhangs or shorter cabinetry. A raised standard dishwasher is also a convenience for users with flexibility issues or lower back pain. Locating a dishwasher at the end of a cabinet run works best for this arrangement. Dishwasher drawers are an excellent alternative.

Natural cork is soft underfoot, making it a very comfortable aging-in-place flooring option.

Handles are easier to grasp than knobs for older hands. Consider them for your cabinets, entry doors, and faucets.

Roll-out trays are ideal for making items on lower shelves more accessible for aging backs and eyes.

Defining a Design Starting Point

Although the architecture of this 1920s home in the Laurel Heights section of San Francisco is considered Classic Modern, there was nothing classic or modern about the space. The homeowners loved the house when they bought it but knew it would need a great deal of updating. The cramped, dark, closed-off kitchen was one of its biggest problems.

A typical challenge on a project of this scope is establishing a design starting point, which then becomes the unifying element for the aesthetic choices that need to be made. One of the details the homeowners loved was the home's barn-style garage doors. They knew they wanted a sliding-door pantry in their kitchen (to enhance traffic flow with its sliding access), so they had one of the garage doors cut to serve that new purpose.

The dark finish of the former garage door is echoed on the painted maple island and industrial-style stools, and its simple lines are carried through the cabinetry's Shaker-style doors and moldings. The pendants, fixtures, and stainless steel appliances pay homage to the pantry door's distinctive hardware.

In making the sliding door the primary focal point of the kitchen, the homeowners incorporated white oak flooring, latte-colored gloss paint on the perimeter cabinets, pale olive backsplash tile, and white wall paint, all designed to complement the dark finish without competing with it.

San Francisco is a city better known for its fog than sun, and the finishes in this kitchen speak to those foggy hues. Its architecture, however, was carefully planned to bring in the cherished rays that beam between the clouds, thanks to a raised ceiling with skylight, which brings in more natural light than the property-line window restrictions allowed.

above · This updated kitchen got more than a style makeover. A skylight added much-needed natural light that limited window options couldn't, and a reworked floor plan gave the space a much stronger connection to adjacent rooms.

left · Well-constructed drawers with dovetailed joinery and full-extension, soft-close glides are ideal for durable, fully accessible storage.

Repurposed garage door
slides across pantry

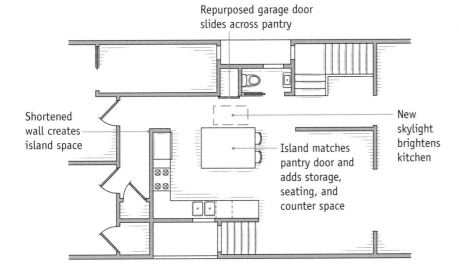

Shortened
wall creates
island space

New
skylight
brightens
kitchen

Island matches
pantry door and
adds storage,
seating, and
counter space

above left · By sliding, rather than swinging open, the pantry door keeps hallway traffic in and out of the kitchen clear.

above right · The oversize pantry door, repurposed from the garage, provided the kitchen's design starting point. Its dark wood tones and simple square lines inspired many of the other design choices in the room.

Developing Your Budget

How much you spend on your kitchen will be based on a number of factors. If you're building a new home or embarking on a whole-house remodel, the kitchen will be budgeted as part of your overall per-square-foot spending allowance.

Otherwise, your project dollars will be dedicated primarily or exclusively to your kitchen. It's not uncommon, even in these scenarios, for a portion of the budget to extend to a neighboring room. Common examples include countertop material and flooring extending into an adjacent room and window ledges or backsplash tile re-covering old fireplace surrounds.

It's important to remember that your new kitchen is an investment and should reflect your home's value, prevailing neighborhood standards, and the scope of changes you plan on making. Under-investing can be as costly a mistake as over-investing.

These are the major items to consider:

- **Cabinetry:** Can consume a large part of your kitchen investment.

- **Appliances:** Another major budget item.

- **Countertops:** Typically a sizable purchase, especially when considering popular engineered or natural stone choices.

- **Flooring:** Costs add up quickly, particularly when you're expanding the flooring from the kitchen into other rooms around it, as often happens during an open-plan remodel.

- **Labor:** Costs vary widely from one region of the country to another and will greatly impact your budget, especially if you're relocating or adding plumbing or electrical components and tearing down walls.

These are additional items to budget, and their cost can add up faster than you think:

- **Sinks and faucets:** Vary widely in price, based on both quality and features.

- **New lighting:** This will increase functionality and add to your investment. It may also be impacted by new local energy-saving code requirements.

- **Backsplash surfacing:** Can be simple and affordable or elaborate and expensive, depending on your taste.

- **Cabinetry hardware:** If required for your door style, the cost needs to be budgeted in.

- **Incidentals:** Drains, soap dispensers, and replacement garbage disposals will also show up on your needs list. Though each is small, the combination will have an impact on your budget, especially in a two-sink kitchen.

Here are three frequently overlooked budget items:

- Surprises hiding behind your walls or beneath discarded flooring can impact your well-planned budget. Factor in 10 to 15 percent for the unexpected.

- Meals during those phases of the remodeling process when you won't have access to your kitchen can hit your household budget, if not your remodeling dollars. Some homeowners are fortunate enough to stay in a second home while the work is being done. Others use an outdoor kitchen in the meantime, save for restaurant meals and convenience foods, or make do in another area of the home.

- Fees can also add up quickly. These could include design, engineering, permit, and loan charges, for example.

above • Details like stacked crown molding and a decorative ventilation hood enclosure add tremendously to your kitchen's style. They also add significantly to the cost of your cabinets and installation.

left • The appliances you choose will have a major impact on your kitchen budget. Choose them with an eye to your household's daily needs, your home's value, and neighborhood standards.

Assembling Your Team

Which professionals you call on for a kitchen remodel will be determined by the scope of work you want to have done.

ARCHITECT

Call an architect first if your new kitchen will be part of a home addition. If you're building new, you will almost always hire an architect or design/build firm. These professionals will guide you on the best ways to achieve harmony between the new and old parts of the house. They will bring in kitchen professionals to provide cabinetry, appliances, and other selections involved, and a builder or general contractor, if not on staff, to execute and coordinate the execution of the design.

DESIGN/BUILD FIRM

Large-scale kitchen remodels involving an older home or major structural changes sometimes use a design/build firm. These companies incorporate a builder or general contractor and in-house design services. The latter could be an architect, interior designer, kitchen designer, or a combination of those talents.

top right • The bright open feel of this space is enhanced by the lack of dividing wall between the kitchen and breakfast room. Including matching cabinetry and tops in that area creates a cohesive look.

right • This modern kitchen has strong lines, pro-level appliances, and a solid U-shaped plan. Pops of color can be added with floor, wall, and window coverings.

KITCHEN DESIGNER

Call a kitchen designer first if you're planning a new kitchen within the current footprint of your home. These professionals will guide you expertly on space planning, integrating the new kitchen with your existing house, and product selections. A designer may also call in a general contractor to finalize the budget and execute the plan.

OTHER PROFESSIONALS

A kitchen designer, interior designer, or decorator can help if you're planning a cosmetic facelift to update the look of the room. A handyman or specialized tradesperson, such as a tile installer, painter, plumber, carpenter, or electrician, may be all that's needed to install the desired changes. Any work affecting the home's plumbing, electrical, or ventilation systems should be handled by a licensed professional. Before undertaking any project, check with your local building department to see what's required in your area.

The exposed duct and trusses enhance the open, architectural feel of this modern kitchen.

LAYOUTS

Before you buy a stick of cabinetry or a single section of countertop, before you choose appliances, fixtures, or flooring, you'll be determining the layout of your kitchen. How your workspaces and storage are planned are the most important decisions you'll make.

THAT WORK

Making Your Existing Footprint Work

One of the best ways to make your remodeling budget stretch further is to work with your existing footprint; that is, the current layout of walls, entries, cabinets, and appliances. This is especially true for your kitchen's ventilation and plumbing. Changes to both of these require professional tradesmen and can entail roof, wall, and floor restructuring. Homes that sit on a concrete slab require another kind of tradesman and this can mean additional labor and expense.

In addition, if your home has flooring that extends from the kitchen through another room, you might want to preserve as much of that flooring as possible by keeping the kitchen's existing footprint. Although flooring in the kitchen can be changed and still work well with connecting spaces (see pp. 146–147 and pp. 162–163 for a few examples), adding in the cost for replacing the floor will add to your budget as well.

Limiting footprint changes doesn't mean your kitchen's style and functionality can't be improved. A span of overly narrow base door cabinets can be replaced with more serviceable, wider pan-drawer cabinets, for instance. An unnecessarily large sink base cabinet chosen by the builder for its affordability can be slimmed down, giving way to a more practical trash pull-out or to conveniently located cutting board storage. Consider upgrading your appliances, borrowing space if needed from adjacent cabinet runs.

Some kitchens have perfectly functional layouts but suffer from style fatigue. If yours falls into this category, update cabinets with new pulls, add countertop corbels to support new stone tops, and use moldings to hide new task and accent lighting.

above • Replacing an existing range with one with a warming drawer and swapping a standard microwave for a model with convection give you four appliances in the same footprint as two.

left • Open-front cabinets, bare windows, a new tile backsplash, and decorative pendants all update the style of a kitchen without expensive footprint changes.

above • Specialty cabinets like a pull-out trash bin near the sink, wide drawer banks, and decorative panels are all upgrades you can make within your existing footprint.

Changing the Footprint

Many remodeling projects do involve footprint changes, large or small. Smaller changes typically leave the existing walls and doorways in place, even gas lines and sink plumbing, but add second sinks, move a refrigerator or dishwasher, open a pass through, or convert a full-height wall to a half-wall.

The largest-scale renovation projects involve considerably more time, investment, skill sets, and knowledge to achieve. They also come with a greater potential for inconvenience and risk. You will be unable to use your kitchen for a longer time when its electrical, plumbing, ventilation, structural members, and flooring are being worked on. You'll have more tradespeople and professionals coming through your home. And you're also more likely to encounter costly surprises along the way as walls are laid bare to problems you didn't know existed behind them.

Sometimes a footprint change is tied into a room-addition project, where a new kitchen will expand into a screened porch, garage, or outdoor space. Whenever rooflines or load-bearing walls are impacted, it is best to work with an architect and engineer. The payoffs for retaining these professional services will be an addition that maintains your home's design and structural integrity, both key to maintaining their long-term value. Your kitchen remodel should always improve your overall home, not just the one room.

below • Removing a wall separating kitchen from eating area is one of the most popular footprint changes and often creates space for an island or peninsula with seating.

left • Tall cabinets and appliances, like the refrigerator and double ovens shown here, are often relocated next to each other in a footprint change to create longer countertop runs around them.

below • Framing a newly opened entry between a kitchen and living areas updates an older home while preserving its traditional style.

Questions and Answers before Making a Change

This San Diego Craftsman-style home had ample charm but hadn't shared any of it with its dated, poorly organized kitchen. The homeowners had four key questions they brought to the design process:

- Could they profoundly improve their kitchen's functionality?

- Could they improve the kitchen's storage without increasing the size of their home?

- Could they create a timeless design, using quality materials, that would deliver a kitchen that would look great and work well for 20 to 25 years?

- Could a remodel significantly increase their enjoyment of the space?

The kitchen that came with the 1920s house certainly wasn't meeting their needs. It felt more like a service room than a space that would nurture their love for healthy cooking and family gatherings. Not only was it old and ugly, but its countertops were too shallow, its wall cabinets too high, and its three entrances awkwardly located.

Changing the layout was essential for allowing the homeowners to enjoy their kitchen as they intended. The new design, which only slightly increased the room's square footage by relocating an interior wall, reorganized the kitchen into efficient work zones. It also dramatically improved traffic flow by rerouting the room's original entries.

The cooking zone encompasses an energy-efficient induction cooktop, a vent hood (which was sorely lacking in the old kitchen), and pull-outs for keeping cooking supplies at point of use.

The wet zone integrates the sink, dishwasher, pull-outs for chopping boards, and 8 feet of servingware storage for

above left · Continuous, integral handles create a streamlined look in the kitchen and eliminate annoying clothing catches on handles or knobs.

above right · Hideaway toekick storage maximizes typically unused space in this compact kitchen. These extra inches are ideal for items not used on a regular basis.

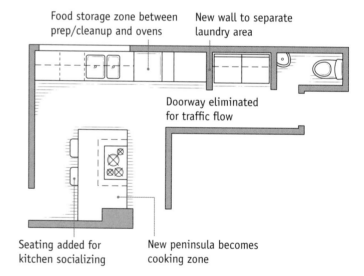

Food storage zone between prep/cleanup and ovens

New wall to separate laundry area

Doorway eliminated for traffic flow

Seating added for kitchen socializing

New peninsula becomes cooking zone

convenient dishwasher unloading. It also includes energy-saving task lighting for the workspace below.

The storage zone hides the paneled, counter-depth refrigerator/freezer, extra space above it for lesser-used, oversize items, and an adjacent pull-out pantry for packaged food.

This new kitchen is well on its way to serving the homeowners efficiently and stylishly for the next two decades.

The improved footprint of this kitchen maximized traffic flow in and out of the room and created new, efficient work zones.

Roll-out trays make base storage more accessible and useful. They can even be used for small appliances and specialty items that don't need to take up counter space.

Deep, wide drawers in the cooking zone are convenient for storing pots and pans right where they'll be used.

The New Work Zones

Early-20th-century kitchen planning created the work triangle. It was based on locating the sink, refrigerator, and cooking appliance (there was only one at that time) in a way that provided an economy of steps for the home cook. As kitchens started to grow larger and more important in the daily life of the household, the work triangle got more and more strained.

Increasingly inflated islands bisected it. New appliances like microwave ovens and dishwashers needed to be factored into the triangle. More recently, second dishwashers, second sinks, and second refrigerators began appearing. The net effect has been to make the original work triangle obsolete. Today's kitchens are zoned around how the space is used. These are the essential zones:

- **Cooking:** The cooking zone encompasses the cooktop (and ovens if not part of the cooktop) or range, vent hood, a microwave and/or steam oven, and storage for cooking gear. It may also have its own sink, trash receptacle, and pot filler.

- **Prep/clean-up:** It incorporates the primary sink; dishwasher; dish, glass, and utensil storage; counter space for meal preparation; trash and perhaps recycling receptacle; and storage for prep and clean-up gear.

- **Food storage:** This zone always includes the home's primary refrigerator and dry-food pantry. It may also incorporate storage for food containers and wraps. The microwave could be located in the food storage zone, given its convenience to the refrigerator and freezer, instead of in the cooking zone. This decision should be based on how the household uses the appliance.

These are potential specialty zones:

- **Baking:** An avid baker may request a baking zone, with a mixer lift, specialized storage for rolling pins, cookie cutters, and other baking essentials, convection oven, stone top for rolling dough, and tray dividers for baking sheets.

- **Health:** Your island can be your health station, incorporating a refrigerator drawer for salad fixings, a filtered dispenser at the

A large, durable sink is the cornerstone of your prep/clean-up zone. Sinks with accessory options help you customize your zone to your daily needs.

sink for fresh water on demand, an outlet and storage space for your juicer, a compost bucket for scraps for your garden, and a steam oven for preparing healthy meals.

- **Kid-friendly:** Many families are creating spaces for their children to safely use the kitchen, with a beverage refrigerator or refrigerator drawers; a microwave drawer; storage for the children's snacks, dishes, and cups; and counter- or chair-height seating for homework and meal preparation help.

- **Entertaining:** Parties always end up in the kitchen, but now many start there, too. Most party zones will incorporate a second sink, which can be used to prepare treats and hold ice when guests arrive. They could also include a self-help beverage fridge and ice maker, storage for servingware, an outlet for blenders, and perhaps even a built-in coffee system. If they're island-based, they will most likely include seating.

- **Homework:** Many parents want to keep the family computer in an easily viewed spot. A designated homework center in the kitchen can be an ideal solution. This zone could also be used for managing bills, shopping lists, and the family calendar. A homework zone should include space for a desktop or laptop computer, power outlets and lights, a comfortable work chair, and potentially file drawers and cubbies for paper storage and office supplies.

A beverage fridge is ideal for both kid-friendly islands and entertaining islands, depending upon the appliance features you choose.

A second sink for party prep tasks and ice storage can be a great entertaining zone enhancement.

Pull-out pantries are ideal for the cooking zone, where they can hold olive oils and cooking sprays where they'll be easily accessible.

A microwave installed in a base cabinet or island is ideal for a kid-friendly zone. One with convection capabilities adds an extra oven to the kitchen.

An Enhanced Kitchen Island

Builders and designers often incorporate islands solely because they're popular. They offer home-owners generic storage capacity and possibly an appliance or sink. But islands hold tremendous potential for helping you carve out increased functionality or even a personal hobby in an all-purpose kitchen.

Your island can form its own essential work zone, with all of the appliances, fixtures, and storage needed to optimize it in one convenient, step-saving location. It could alternatively serve as a specialized work center, depending on your space, preferences, and budgets.

Converting an existing generic island into an enhanced work center, or just adding new features, is typically easier than creating a new island. Adding counter-height seating could take advantage of extra floor space and existing cabinetry for a kid-friendly or party zone. Your new countertops would extend 15 inches beyond the cabinets for a one-level countertop, 12 inches beyond a new kneewall for a raised bar; both options will likely call for overhang supports.

To add an island to an existing kitchen, you need enough floor space for both new cabinetry and work aisles around it and more if you're adding seating. You also want your island to be well proportioned to the kitchen surrounding it.

Although many local building codes specify a minimum of 36 inches for walking space, you'll find that this is too cramped for kitchen work. A work aisle should be a minimum of 42 inches for a single-cook kitchen and 48 inches for two cooks. The island itself is likely to be a minimum of 2 feet, the standard depth of kitchen cabinetry. If you have this space

top • Whatever style or functional enhancements you choose for your island, be sure you have enough room to walk or work around it.

above • Open storage on the end of an island creates a stylish and convenient display for cookbooks, household items in decorative containers, or collectibles.

available, you can add functionality with specialized storage and appliances and even add style with a coordinating finish or countertop, rather than matching what's on the perimeter. (Coordinating is often easier than matching older finishes.)

If you don't have space for an island, a mobile kitchen cart can be a good stand-in, as long as you have floor space to store it when it's not being used.

left • Islands are ideal for locating the increasing array of undercounter appliances available today. Some worth considering are ice maker, wine captain, microwave, and refrigerator drawers.

below • One of the most popular island enhancements is seating, but it requires room behind it for walking space and should never be located on the working side of a range or cooktop-facing aisle.

The Family Landing Zone

Kitchens and countertops attract clutter. It's a fact of the modern junk-mail-run, electronics-driven, multitasking life that this suburban Philadelphia household was determined to conquer in their recent remodel.

To keep the handsome new granite tops from being buried in paperwork, they created a landing zone convenient to both their garage door and front entry. Its base cabinetry provides space for briefcases and bags. Its clever wall cabinet keeps keys, chargers, mail, messages, and a few personal necessities close at hand yet out of sight.

The long countertop shared by the wet bar does double duty. The end near the sink holds items necessary when entertaining guests, whereas the section below the message center is large enough to hold a decorative basket—even multiples, if they wish—for each family member, to collect the individual's daily items. Baskets like these can be easily tucked out of sight when company comes.

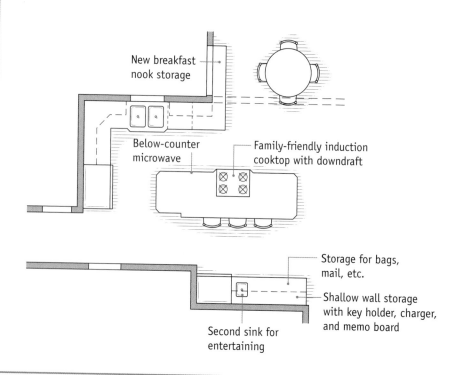

New breakfast nook storage

Below-counter microwave

Family-friendly induction cooktop with downdraft

Storage for bags, mail, etc.

Shallow wall storage with key holder, charger, and memo board

Second sink for entertaining

top • The dining table, chairs, and chandelier coordinate handsomely with the wood-stained and painted black cabinetry for a cohesive look.

above • The new family landing zone incorporated a message center for keys, notes, and personal electronics charging.

right • The new island maximized workability with a microwave and cooktop and plenty of storage and countertop surface around them.

below • Base storage in the family landing zone keeps purses, backpacks, and briefcases out of the traffic zone, convenient for coming and going, but tucked out of sight otherwise.

above • The sunny breakfast nook incorporates ample storage, making both kitchen table homework and family dining convenient.

Creating an Open-Plan Kitchen

Because kitchens are the new living rooms of our homes—they're where we eat, drink coffee with friends, do homework, review bills, and hold family conferences—they increasingly take center stage. The walls that have separated them from the rest of the living space have come down figuratively and literally.

This has entailed a rethinking in the design of the open-plan kitchen. Traffic flow needs to be routed around, not through, cooking zones. Refrigeration and pantry foods should be accessible to the chef but also to other members of the household and guests. Kitchen visitors should be clear of hot pots and pans.

The kitchen's ventilation needs to be sufficient for the specified cooking equipment so that the living spaces next to it, or diners seated at the end of the island, aren't overcome by food gases or steam.

top • Open-plan kitchens with multiple seating areas maximize interaction between guests and hosts and improve traffic flow between work space and entertainment space.

right • Modern European-inspired kitchens often hide appliances behind cabinetry doors for an "un-kitchen" open-plan loft style.

Many homeowners prefer that their kitchens blend completely with the living spaces around them. Integrated appliances featuring cabinetry fronts, with ventilation tucked behind matching millwork, have long been a popular way of creating this effect, creating an "un-kitchen" or "hidden" kitchen look. Newer, European-inspired offerings include island countertops that slide closed to hide sinks and retracting faucets and cabinetry doors that slide in front of ovens and other appliances.

If creating a hidden kitchen is your goal, you'll want to strongly factor in the architecture, style, and major finishes of the surrounding rooms in your remodel plans. The finishes hiding your kitchen storage and appliances take on even greater importance when they're the sole focal point in that space. It's critical that they work seamlessly with the major elements in the rooms opening onto the kitchen. Unless you're after the rare eclectic style, you're going to stay traditional or modern, depending on what's in the open living space.

Some open-plan kitchens put professional-style appliances—especially ranges and hoods—on display as a focal point.

Phasing in Footprint Improvements

You can update your kitchen without a full-scale remodel or footprint changes. You can even update it in phases, as your schedule and budget allow. Improve your storage without replacing your cabinets. Replace appliances individually or in a suite for more savings. Update your sink and faucet when you change your countertops to improve functionality in your prep/clean-up zone. (Tops are often done last so that the new cooktop's cutout or slide-in range can be factored into the template.)

If you need additional storage capacity, you have two solid strategies that avoid remodeling. First, maximize the cabinets you already have with interior accessories. There are numerous types available to expand the storage capacity of your kitchen cabinets so that you don't have to expand your space. These include making better use of a blind corner cabinet with a swing-out accessory that makes the back section usable; using a two-tiered organizer to add extra drawer capacity; replacing a builder-grade base-cabinet half shelf with a full-depth roll-out tray; or converting a narrow cabinet to a more usable tray base with tall dividers.

Second, look for untapped storage opportunities on your walls or ceiling with a pot rack and on your backsplash with a rail-based organizing system. Even toekick drawers can add secret storage.

If your appliances are outdated, you can replace them with more technologically advanced, feature-rich, energy- or water-saving models that fit in the same space. An example would be swapping out an inefficient electric cooktop for an induction model.

The bottom line is this: By working with what you have, and doing what you can with the resources available to you, you can minimize your kitchen investment while improving its functionality and style over time.

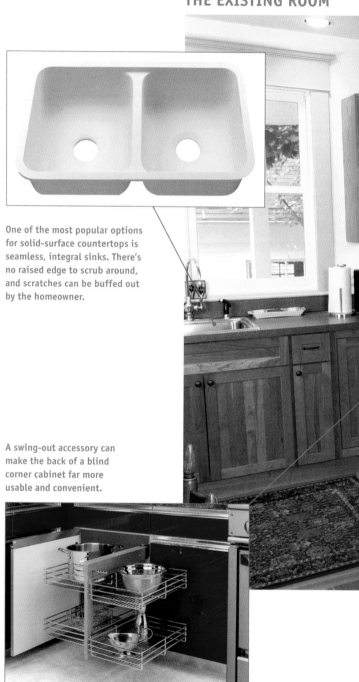

One of the most popular options for solid-surface countertops is seamless, integral sinks. There's no raised edge to scrub around, and scratches can be buffed out by the homeowner.

A swing-out accessory can make the back of a blind corner cabinet far more usable and convenient.

A backsplash
organizer system
adds flexible storage
options to the
kitchen in otherwise
untapped space.

A solid-surface
countertop offers a
smooth work area
and repairability
not available in
other surfaces.

above • You can improve a dated kitchen's style and functionality in
phases, rather than all at once, if your schedule and budget make
this a better solution.

A Compact, Contemporary Family Kitchen

When he relocated to San Diego, the architect decided the mid-size, mid-century home in a coastal community would work well for his small family, but the kitchen would definitely need work. He wanted updated appliances and fixtures, a more functional family-friendly layout with seating, and a better connection to the adjacent living area. The kitchen also needed to reflect his contemporary style, which the original didn't.

The new plan gave the family a zoned kitchen. It features deep drawers for pots and pans near the new range top, an island clean-up station with dishwasher and deep sink, and a food-storage area with fridge, pull-out pantry, and nearby ovens. At the end of the peninsula, separating the kitchen from the dining area, is a wine fridge that can be accessed without interrupting kitchen work.

The layout included the desired seating as well as an electronics-charging station on the back of the island. Both make schoolwork and working at home convenient in this well-used space. The quartz countertop helps keep it low maintenance.

Style was not overlooked in the new, family-friendly plan. Glossy white cabinets with continuous integrated handles, a sleek gray backsplash, and gray oak floors provide the clean design quotient the architect sought in this updated kitchen.

top • A wine fridge at the end of the peninsula allows visitors to select a bottle without interrupting the kitchen's work flow.

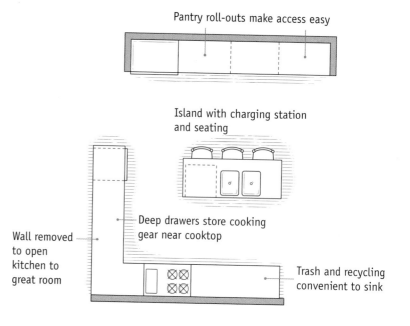

Pantry roll-outs make access easy

Island with charging station and seating

Deep drawers store cooking gear near cooktop

Wall removed to open kitchen to great room

Trash and recycling convenient to sink

left · The kitchen's new layout allowed space for a family-friendly island with electronic charging stations and seating, a pro-style range top, and convenient work zones.

above · Removing a wall created the opportunity for a long peninsula that opens to the great room and its ocean views.

left · Interior accessories like roll-out trays and drawer organizers maximize the storage potential of this kitchen. Glassware storage is convenient to both the full-size and wine refrigerators.

CABINETS

Cabinets are the largest, most visible, and potentially most expensive purchase in your kitchen. Your choices are incredibly varied and influenced by your needs and tastes, budget, and floor plan.

Framed versus Frameless Cabinets

Cabinets with face frames—strips of finished wood that attach to the front of a cabinet—are the standard in many American homes. Frameless cabinets are relatively new to this market but have been popular in Europe for years. There are pros and cons to each type.

FRAMED

Framed cabinets are a traditional style and work well in most kitchens. They are easiest for many installers to work with, in part because they've been working with this type of installation system for decades. This could translate to a quicker, better, and more affordable installation.

Framed cabinets allow for style choices not achievable with frameless models. The most significant stylistically is the ability to include inset doors, a look in which the doors and drawer fronts close flush with the cabinet's face frame. The second, more subtle detail is the option to extend the face frame for a more seamless look when applying decorative details to the cabinets or ending bank of cabinets, also called a run.

Because wider framed cabinets need a face frame divider, known as a stile, access to the interior can be a bit limited. They also have narrower drawers than frameless because of the face frame allowance. Including full-extension drawer glides, choosing cabinets that accept butt doors that don't require stiles, and adding interior accessories like roll-out trays can help offset these shortcomings.

top · The continuous integrated handles seen on the island are a custom, frameless cabinet upgrade.

above · Inset doors and drawers are a higher-end style available on framed, usually custom, cabinets.

FRAMELESS

Unlike framed cabinets, frameless cabinets allow you full access to the cabinet's interior by eliminating the obstruction of a face frame. This gives drawers and roll-out trays more storage potential and accessibility, especially in wider cabinets that might have a center stile if they were framed. Frameless cabinets also use full-overlay doors, which offer a more appealing look to many buyers than the partial-overlay doors that come with some affordable framed cabinets. And unlike standard framed cabinets, frameless wall cabinets offer flush bottoms, making it easier to install fewer, longer undercabinet lights.

Frameless cabinets also use less wood than framed cabinets, creating a more eco-friendly kitchen. They can be shipped unassembled, which means less storage space is required for them until they're needed, but unassembled cabinets incur costlier installation, as they need to be put together before they can be installed.

top • Full-overlay slab door styles are available in both framed and frameless cabinet lines.

left • Full-overlay door styles are often pricier than their partial overlay equivalents.

Cabinetry

Cabinets are typically made in small, local shops or in large North American, Asian, or European factories. Where they originate doesn't determine whether they're custom, semi-custom, or stock, though most stock cabinets are factory-made here or abroad. A kitchen made in a local cabinet shop will often use doors and accessories from stock sources, thus limiting their potential to offer true custom cabinetry. A high-end factory, on the other hand, may have an internal woodworking team able to do complete customization.

Local shops are sometimes constrained by environmental regulations from offering certain types of spray finishes that offer maximum durability or ultra high gloss. They may also lack the sophisticated machinery required for building curved cabinets.

The cabinet supplier you select should tell you where your cabinets are being built, how much customization and what finishes are available, and whether they address any environmental concerns you have. You'll want these questions answered before you pay a deposit that may not be refundable.

Features like inset doors and seamlessly stacked cabinets are hallmarks of fine custom-framed cabinetry.

STOCK
$

- Most affordable cabinetry option.
- Widely available in most areas, either on store shelves or delivered in 1 to 3 weeks.
- Cost-cutting construction and materials are common, as are limited warranties.
- Limited sizes mean increased use of filler strips during installation, potentially robbing storage.
- Limited selection and lack of modifications make them unsuitable for some projects.
- Typically available in oak, maple, and cherry veneers, as well as very basic laminates and thermofoils.

SEMI-CUSTOM
$$

- Large selection of styles, sizes, configurations, and finishes available for most projects.
- Most commonly framed cabinetry.
- Excellent design flexibility allows for some depth changes, as well as style enhancements like valances, flush furniture sides, beaded backs, and decorative toekicks built into the cabinetry.
- Wide selection of accessories and moldings available.
- Typically available in oak and quartersawn oak, cherry, maple, birch, hickory, and painted or glazed finishes.
- Usually ship in 4 to 6 weeks.
- Usually offer excellent warranties.

CUSTOM
$$$

- Widest selection of style and finish offerings, including exotic woods and high-end laminates.
- Offer ability to customize cabinet size, type, and shape, based on designer's drawings.
- Offer potential for color-matching to a paint sample.
- Create opportunity for designing a unique door style from a wide selection of molding and edge options.
- Offer potential for mixing finishes within one cabinet, such as a contrasting back or interior.
- Allow for inclusion of custom carvings and moldings.
- Most environmentally friendly cabinets are custom lines.
- Usually ship in 6 to 12 weeks.

The pairing of a distressed, painted finish and inset door style creates old-world style for a custom cabinet investment.

A contemporary kitchen like this can be affordably created using full-overlay, frameless stock cabinets.

Construction Matters

How a cabinet is assembled, and from what materials, has an impact on how well it will hold up to the rigors of a busy kitchen.

Engineered woods, including particleboard, have gotten an undeserved bad reputation because of poor-quality grades selected by some manufacturers in the past. Today, there are waterproof particleboards or furniture boards that won't be damaged as quickly or easily by a leak and that have minimal formaldehyde-based offgassing. These materials are especially common today in European cabinetry imports. Engineered-wood cabinets typically have an easy-clean, nonporous melamine interior that doesn't harbor bacteria.

Medium-density fiberboard, commonly known as MDF, is a very stable engineered-wood product that is ideal for cabinet shelves and painted, recessed-door-style center panels, as it will remain relatively stable in humid climates. On shelves, that means little to no warping, and on doors, few to no joint separation issues.

Custom cabinet boxes are typically made from ¾-inch plywood. Plywood is an upgrade option on most semicustom cabinets (often in a slimmer ⅝-inch thickness), with an engineered-wood box being standard. The side panels of wood-species cabinets are generally clad in wood veneer. Custom cabinets tend to have the highest-quality, most-durable veneers.

Drawer construction is a major consideration in choosing cabinetry. Dovetailed joinery has become the quality standard for traditional cabinetry. Cabinets that are dovetailed on all four corners offer more stability than those with front-only dovetails. Stapled drawers, as you often find on stock cabinetry, offer the least durability.

Contemporary kitchen cabinets, particularly those from Europe, increasingly feature metal drawer boxes that coordinate well with the cabinet's exteriors.

above • Metal drawer boxes are a popular feature in modern frameless cabinets. Semi-custom and custom lines offer full-extension, soft-close glides.

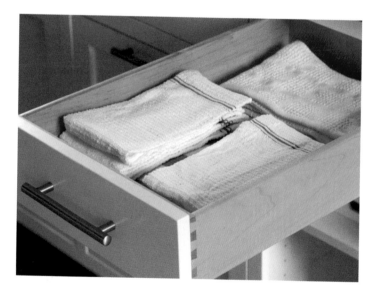

above • Dovetailed joinery is a durable drawer construction method commonly available in semi-custom and custom cabinets.

above · Smooth, flush furniture ends, as seen on the wall cabinet, are available today on semi-custom and custom cabinets.

left · Custom cabinetry is typically constructed with durable plywood sides, full-extension soft-close drawer glides, and soft-close doors.

Reface or Renew

A common kitchen remodeling question is whether to keep or get rid of your cabinets. Not all updates require you to eliminate them, and many green designers will look for ways to keep them out of landfills. There are several points to consider to guide you on this major piece of your kitchen update.

First, check to see if the cabinets are in sound structural condition. If they aren't, then they should be replaced. If they're in good condition but not meeting your storage or style preferences, they can be updated with storage accessories and decorative changes.

If your cabinets are structurally sound and you want to keep them—perhaps because you like the countertop sitting on top of them—but want to update their look, then you have two choices: reface or renew/refurbish. It's important to know, though, that either of these choices will lock you into the kitchen's existing footprint.

In the refacing process, doors, moldings, and drawer fronts are replaced with new versions; side panels, toekicks, and face frames, if your cabinets aren't frameless, are covered with matching skins.

Many refacing companies offer interior accessories that can greatly enhance the storage capacity and functionality of your existing cabinets, and new hardware can give your new doors and drawers an updated look. Refacing is often less expensive and more environmentally friendly than replacing cabinets because no demolition is required and your cabinet boxes are reused.

A less-expensive alternative is to have your existing cabinets refinished. This is the most affordable alternative but offers only cosmetic improvements. Exposed hinges can be replated or replaced to coordinate with the new cabinet finish and knobs or pulls can be updated for more visual impact. A paint expert can do this work, though it's something many do-it-yourselfers can also tackle. However, although your cabinets may look like new when the work is done, the functionality will remain unchanged unless you also take on an accessory-installation project.

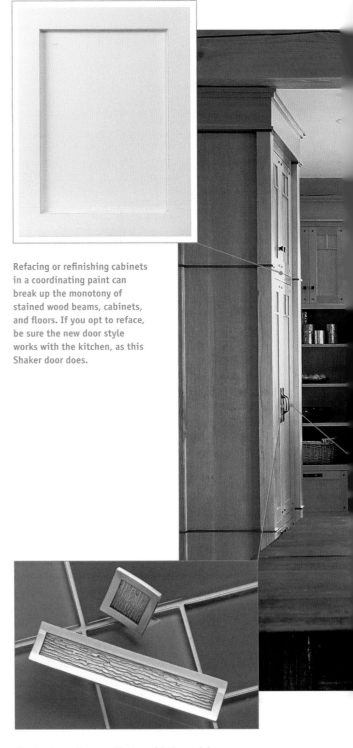

Refacing or refinishing cabinets in a coordinating paint can break up the monotony of stained wood beams, cabinets, and floors. If you opt to reface, be sure the new door style works with the kitchen, as this Shaker door does.

New hardware that coordinates with the stainless-steel appliances and faucet can quickly and affordably update a kitchen. Just choose handle styles that match the existing hardware holes.

THE EXISTING ROOM

Cabinets that are in very good condition, with functional storage, are ideal candidates for refacing or refurbishing to give the kitchen a new look.

Interior accessories can increase the usable storage and accessibility of your existing cabinets. They can be added long after your cabinets were installed for new functionality.

Hardware can also be chosen to match other finishes in the room—like the dining room chandelier. The dark finish beautifully complements painted white cabinet finishes.

"Green" Cabinets

Some homeowners choose eco-friendly cabinets because of their sustainability. Some brands feature certification logos like Forest Stewardship Council (FSC), U.S. Green Building Council member, or Environmental Stewardship Program (ESP).

As the number of certifying organizations and certifications (many affiliated with trade associations) grows, so does confusion. A cabinet may be from a sustainably harvested forest that doesn't have FSC certification. Or it may carry ESP certification, meaning minimal formaldehyde emissions, but have a greater impact on the environment from being trucked across country. The important details to ask your designer or supplier if you're concerned about sustainability include the following:

- Where are the cabinets made and how will they be transported to my job site?

- Are they from a sustainable or renewable source?

- Do their materials or production processes harm the environment?

- Can they be recycled in the future if I wish to remodel?

If you or your family members have serious health issues, look for eco-friendly cabinets that are "healthier" than others. These include the following:

- Cabinets that exceed international air-quality standards for low or no VOCs (volatile organic compounds). This typically means they use water-based stains and paints.

- Construction from plywood, particleboard, and MDF that has no urea formaldehyde. This, too, is to eliminate dangerous offgassing.

- Assembly with nontoxic, no- or low-VOC adhesives.

Cabinets made from sustainable, responsibly harvested wood sources may look like any other but are more eco-friendly.

top and bottom right · Eco-friendly cabinets that are healthier for the planet and your home can fit any style kitchen. A natural finish that can be restored to its original beauty contributes to a cabinet's sustainability.

facing page bottom · Cabinets finished with no (or minimal) VOCs are safer for indoor environments, including your kitchen.

Wood-Species Characteristics

Too often, homeowners select wood cabinets without considering their natural characteristics. Wood, like the trees it came from, is not uniform or perfect. Its beauty lies in its flaws and variations. Understanding what is characteristic of each species will help you choose wisely for your home. These are the most widely available.

MAPLE

This relatively even wood typically has a straight, subtle grain, and it can run yellow or pink. It is prone to mineral streaks, which look like dark birth marks on its surface. It stains and paints evenly. In fact, most painted kitchen cabinets use maple as their base.

BIRCH

Like maple, birch has straight, even grain and golden tones. It is sometimes used as a more affordable substitute for maple.

CHERRY

Cherry has dramatic grain variations and contrasts. It is not uncommon to see strawberry blonde tones blending with darker reds in cherry cabinetry. Cherry is also prone to darkening over time with exposure to sunlight. It is a hardwood, but softer than oak or maple.

Cherry is known for its warm tones and strong pattern and color variations. These can be somewhat subdued with a dark stain.

above • An even, closed-grain wood, maple comes in a wide range of light and dark stains.

above • Maple's smooth, hard surface makes it ideal for painted cabinet finishes.

right • Birch shares many of maple's close-grained, blonde qualities, but is generally a more affordable alternative.

ALDER

Cabinets made from alder have reddish-gold tones, but these are less dramatic in their contrasts and variations than cherry. It is sometimes used as a more affordable alternative to cherry in semi-custom and custom cabinet projects. Its softness makes it a popular choice for distressed styles, too.

OAK

The classic oak cabinet has a very strong open grain that offers light-dark contrast and cathedral-like detail. Oak can be rift-cut or quartersawn for a more even appearance and elimination of the cathedral style that some people dislike. This variation generally costs considerably more than standard oak and is rarely available in stock cabinet lines.

HICKORY

This is a nature lover's wood, with its extreme color contrasts and open grain. Although extremely hard, hickory is prone to mineral streaks, bird pecks, and other evidence of its past life as a tree.

top • Hickory is known for its striking grain variations from light to dark. It's most often selected for very rustic country or cabin kitchens.

right • Quartersawn oak comes from the same trees as regular oak, but the even grain and superior stain acceptance resulting from its different cut makes it a premium choice, especially for Craftsman-style projects.

above • Alder is often a more even-toned, affordable substitute for premium cherry.

left • Oak is one of the most widely available, affordable wood species. It's most often used in budget projects and country kitchens.

The New Laminates

When many of us think of laminate cabinets, we picture low-quality, unattractive imitations of natural products peeling off of particleboard doors. In the post–World War II building boom, laminates got a bad name, and it's not uncommon to see these hastily constructed cabinets torn out in remodels.

Newer laminates are largely European in origin but have become increasingly available in the United States and Canada as contemporary cabinet styles grow in appeal. There is no single characteristic of these highly original surfaces; what unites the best of them is their dramatic finish that pays homage to a beloved material without trying too hard to replicate it. Laminate cabinets can bring the look of a premium wood to your kitchen without the premium price tag—or rainforest impact—but can't be refinished or even easily repaired, if damaged. Better materials, manufacturing processes, and adhesives in these man-made products have made them more durable than in their early years, though. They're better looking now, too.

These new laminate offerings are even more varied than their painted and wood-grain counterparts. Laminates can have any of the following:

- A strong texture that adds a dimensional element to the kitchen beyond color and pattern.

- A translucent glass-like sheen that adds a unique high-gloss element.

- Continuous, book-matched finishes inspired by exotic woods that are otherwise out of budget or largely unavailable. Bookmatching is the cabinetry equivalent of a dress whose pattern extends perfectly across seams.

- Some manufacturers combine two laminates in one cabinet—often solid finishes paired with wood grains—for an artistic, furniture-style design that likely won't be found at the house down the street.

above • Mass production and mass marketing are making these new, improved laminates available at more affordable price points.

above • Seamless style is now available with laminates thanks to realistic-looking wood and book-matched grains across a full cabinet run.

New premium laminates offer the look and texture of exotic species without an inch of rainforest destruction.

Mixing Cabinet Finishes in a Kitchen

The owners of this 1920s Italianate Arts and Crafts home in British Columbia, Canada, love historic European architecture and wanted to incorporate its style into their kitchen remodel. At the same time, the space needed a serious modernization.

There was no cooking ventilation to pair with the new Aga® range, for instance, and the old-world floor plan chopped up the space in ways that didn't work for the homeowners' lifestyle. They remodeled their kitchen to meet their current and future needs but also to honor the historic style they so greatly respect.

The red Aga served as the inspiration for the stained red cabinetry and beadboard backsplash. The creamy finish on the perimeter cabinets lets the red accents be the star. The simple, traditional door styles and similarly styled moldings and decorative detail shared by both unify the space.

A subtle diamond theme shows up in both the white cabinets' lattice uppers and the red cabinets' leaded-glass doors. There are also chunky brackets and toekick corners that appear in both the red and white sections. All of these individual details add up to a space that's vibrant, vintage, and playfully pulled together.

above • The oversize, vintage-style range was the inspiration for the kitchen's color and design scheme.

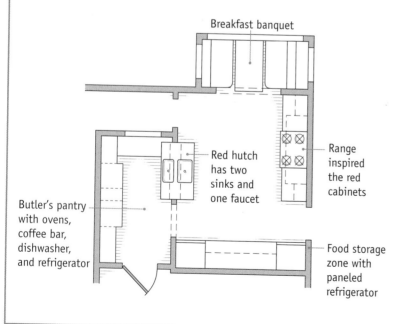

Breakfast banquet

Red hutch has two sinks and one faucet

Range inspired the red cabinets

Butler's pantry with ovens, coffee bar, dishwasher, and refrigerator

Food storage zone with paneled refrigerator

above • The diamond theme, picked up from the glass inserts and tile backsplash detail, is seen here in the door's cut-work center panel.

above • Unifying the two cabinet finishes are decorative details like the arched valance and diamond pattern seen in both the cream and red offerings.

The range's ruby tones are echoed in the painted red cabinetry for a rich counterpoint to the creamy wood, countertops, and tile backsplash.

Interior Accessories

Interior accessories keep the contents of your cabinets organized and accessible. They can even increase the storage capacity of your kitchen. For example, a 15-inch-wide base cabinet with a center shelf can't hold large pots or pans, but with several tray dividers installed in place of the shelf, it can hold numerous flat items like baking sheets, pizza stones, cutting boards, and platters.

The idea here is to be creative and flexible in your thinking to make your cabinets work for your needs. There are many interior accessories to consider when planning your kitchen to maximize the storage spaces you commonly use.

ROLL-OUT TRAYS

These base- and pantry-cabinet inserts make the contents in the back of the cabinet easier to reach. They also increase the storage capacity of any cabinet equipped only with a half-shelf in the middle. However, you will lose some capacity because of the roll-out's sides and possibly glides. Framed cabinets cost you the most space because of the frame itself; ¾ inch on each side multiplied by 24 inches deep adds up. A frameless cabinet will only cost you the roll-out's sides. Undermount glides won't deduct space as side-mounted models do.

top • A two-tiered cutlery insert adds the equivalent of half an extra drawer and keeps your utensils and silverware organized for easy access.

right • A lazy Susan (or super Susan, distinguished by its lack of center pole) make the contents of deep corner cabinets more accessible.

LAZY SUSANS AND SWING-OUTS

Deep corner cabinets with these interior accessories are more accessible than those without them. Lazy Susans typically install in a standard 33-inch or 36-inch base corner cabinet. Super Susans install without a center pole and tend to be a few inches larger. Swing-outs make the back reaches of blind corner cabinets, generally installed next to appliances or sink base cabinets because of space limitations, accessible.

DRAWER ORGANIZERS

Top-drawer units, sized to fit many drawer sizes, can hold knives neatly in an in-drawer block, spices, silverware, and hostess sets. Two-tiered silverware caddies increase the storage capacity of each top drawer, but won't fit in some shallower models. Deep-drawer organizers, made popular by open kitchen plans' reduced wall-cabinet capacity, can hold entire dish sets between flexible pegboard systems and lids near their pots or pans.

TRAY DIVIDERS

Often used to make the hard-to-use space above refrigerators or ovens easier to access, tray dividers can also make narrow base cabinets more useful.

above • A tray divider makes excellent use of narrow spaces for storing large, flat items. Pull-out glides add convenience.

right • Roll-out trays add convenience and accessibility to base and tall cabinet storage.

far right • Pull-out fillers make good use of otherwise dead space for zoned storage, as seen here in this clean-up supply cabinet next to the sink.

TRASH AND RECYCLING PULL-OUTS

Kitchens that are too small for a separate trash cabinet will benefit from a trash pull-out below the sink, if plumbing space allows. Households that recycle will enjoy the convenience of dual pull-outs in the same base storage space on trash day. Depending on its size, these kinds of pull-outs might not fit if you have a garbage disposal.

MIXER LIFT

Large stand mixers can be stored in base cabinets on lifts that bring them to counter height when needed. This frees up valuable counter space and avoids the risk of pulled muscles from lifting these heavy items.

WALL CABINET SHELF PULL-DOWNS

These are increasingly popular among older and wheelchair-bound homeowners who otherwise wouldn't be able to take advantage of standard-height wall cabinets. They also are ideal for anyone who dreads getting on a stepladder to reach items on higher shelves.

top • A mixer lift gives you the convenient option of hiding away your heavy mixer when it's not being used and moving it into place without back strain when you're ready to bake.

right • Wall cabinet pull-downs make hard-to-reach items accessible to wheelchair users and height-challenged homeowners.

left · A tilt-out tray is small but makes good use of otherwise wasted space.

ORGANIZERS FOR UNEXPECTED SPACES

These organizers make use of space you might not otherwise use, thus increasing the storage potential of your cabinetry. Most can be purchased from an accessories manufacturer and are easily installed yourself after your cabinets are already in place.

- **Door storage:** Storage units that mount on the backs of doors can organize cleaning supplies in sink base cabinets or spices in wall cabinets.

- **Pull-outs:** Some replace 3-inch or 6-inch base- or wall-cabinet fillers for small items, taking advantage of otherwise dead space. Larger pull-outs range from 9-inch base or wall cabinets to 18-inch full-height pantries, putting more functional and accessible storage into narrow spaces. These are best ordered with your cabinets, if possible, as removing fillers can damage adjacent cabinets. Their fronts will match your cabinet order; interior components are typically wood or metal, depending on the product line.

- **Tilt-out trays:** These are small, helpful accessories for the otherwise-unused space between sinks and cabinet fronts, converting a false panel to a storage compartment for sponges, scrubbers, drains, and other clean-up items. They're typically made of dishwasher-safe stainless steel or plastic and are easy to remove for cleanup.

- **Sink-base organizers:** Often the cabinet below the kitchen sink holds a hodgepodge of pipes and cleaning supplies. When there's room for them around the sink plumbing, rollout organizers make this large, untapped space far more usable.

left · Pull-out trash and recycling bins built into the cabinets eliminate a common kitchen eyesore.

Decorative Details

Decorative detailing on your cabinets can greatly enhance the appearance of your kitchen—especially if it's traditional or transitional—and take it from drab to fabulous in short order. It can be factored into the planning of a new kitchen or used to refurbish an existing one and should always be in keeping with the overall style of the space in which it's being installed. Here are some options to consider.

DECORATIVE MOLDINGS

Crown molding atop your wall cabinets and a light rail along their bottom edges can add a strong style element to your kitchen. If you're considering it for existing cabinetry you're not going to refinish, it's easiest to coordinate a complementary paint or stain rather than try to achieve an exact match on wood that's already aged.

DECORATIVE FEET OR VALANCES

Transitional or traditional base cabinets can gain style points through the addition of one of these details. Valances can also be applied to open wall cabinets or below them to span an open space above a sink, for example. These decorative elements are easiest to plan into a new purchase because they almost always match the cabinets to which they're attached.

CORBELS AND COUNTERTOP SUPPORTS

Although their main purpose is to hold up heavy countertop overhangs, corbels and other supports can look great while doing their job. They should be sized appropriately for the size of the overhang and professionally installed for safety.

above • Decorative brackets can add interest to wall cabinetry, open shelves, and hearth designs.

above • Crown molding dresses up traditional and transitional cabinets. It's important to choose a style in keeping with the cabinetry and the room.

CAPITALS, FLUTES, OVERLAYS, LEGS, AND ONLAYS

These decorative carvings are commonly found in traditional or transitional kitchens and are almost always planned into their design to allow for clearances and finish matching. Some modern kitchens employ metal or simple matching legs to create a feeling of openness.

DECORATIVE PANELING

A bare cabinet side can look overly plain, and an exposed back will look unfinished. Decorative paneling will dress up these areas and give the kitchen a more pulled-together look. It's typically available in three formats, from least to most expensive: beaded, applied panel, and integral panel. An applied panel adds door fronts and possibly overlays to a bare expanse; integral panels, often available only in custom lines, incorporate the paneling into the overall panel for the richest look.

GLASS DOORS

Glass doors add sparkle and brightness to a kitchen. They can make a space feel more open as well as display decorative contents behind them. Glass-door cabinets are sometimes enhanced by interior lighting and glass shelves. They always have finished interiors, usually matching the exterior, but sometimes contrasting for added drama.

above · Decorative toekick detail and furniture-style legs, chosen to coordinate with the cabinetry's style, can add interest and flair to any kitchen.

left · Glass door inserts brighten up a kitchen and come in a wide array of textures and finishes that work with traditional, transitional, and even modern kitchens.

Knobs, Pulls, Glides, and Hinges

Cabinet hardware includes decorative knobs and pulls, drawer glides, and door hinges. The latter two are as important to the functionality of your kitchen as the first are to its style and accessibility.

Knobs and pulls are the jewelry of your kitchen, and like jewelry, can range from simple and affordable to elaborate and expensive. You can find simple brushed nickel knobs in home center 12-packs for less than $3 per piece or crystal versions from a designer showroom for $30 per piece. If you're paneling your refrigerator, you're going to need even pricier pulls, as they have to be sturdy enough to open that door. It's not uncommon to spend more than $100 apiece on these.

Drawer glides and hinges are your cabinets' workhorses. Although industry standards call for a 50-pound minimum rating on glides, many manufacturers offer heavier-duty 75-pound or higher ratings that will better withstand the rigors of time and family use. The best glides offer undermounted, full-extension capability that make it easier to get items from the back of the drawer, and soft-close motion that protects your cabinets from the wear and tear of slamming.

Soft-close, anti-slamming motion is also becoming increasingly available—and expected—in door hinges. Once exclusive to custom cabinetry, soft-close doors are showing up in more semi-custom and even higher-end stock lines. What has helped this trickle-down luxury is the invention of integral soft-close mechanisms for the hinges, meaning a separate bumper is no longer required to enjoy the soft-close feature. This creates a cleaner looking cabinet and a more affordable offering by the manufacturer.

Although hinges were once considered purely functional, some traditional kitchens are opting for exposed, decorative styles as a design statement. Typically, full-overlay door styles that cover the front of the cabinet almost completely employ hidden hinges. Partial or standard overlay doors, in which more of the cabinet's face frame is exposed, may have hidden or exposed hinges. For inset doors—found almost exclusively on custom cabinets—the hinge is almost always a design feature.

above • Long pulls have become increasingly popular in recent years. They offer sleek style, but are harder to replace in the future when tastes or trends change, as they don't fit standard hole spreads.

above • Decorative cabinet hardware is an easy way to add personal detail to your kitchen, reflecting your taste, interests, and individuality.

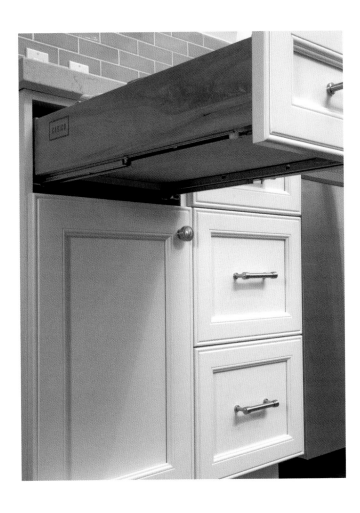

above · Hidden hinges are among the most widely available today and provide easy adjustability for vertical and horizontal door alignment. The newest models integrate soft-close technology.

top left · Undermount glides allow for larger drawer boxes. The best ones offer full-extension opening and soft-closing.

left · Bin pulls are a popular decorative hardware choice for traditional and transitional kitchens.

Enhancing Kitchen Style with Cabinet Details and Hardware

This 1940s Pensacola, Florida, Craftsman began a fabled life as a boarding house and restaurant of some renown. Noted for its fried chicken, the one-time commercial kitchen served famous and local Southern food fans alike.

Its new owners honored the home's past with a vintage-style whole-house remodel and residential conversion. One fact remains the same: Its kitchen is still capable of turning out spectacular meals. Only now it does so with spectacular style, too.

The owners incorporated the original fireplace chimney in the middle of the room as a divider between the remodeled kitchen and a new butler's pantry, selecting finishes that would showcase its rustic charm and complement its strong scale. The upper cabinets at the chimney feature double-sided glass doors to highlight both rooms. The glass is echoed in the top sections of the wall cabinets across the kitchen, evoking harmony and a vintage motif. The glass cabinets also create a feeling of light and airiness in the space.

The custom cabinets with inset doors and classic moldings beautifully reinforce the vintage feel of the kitchen and speak to the rich history of Gulf Coast architecture. Given the scale of the fireplace chimney and room, the island has beefier legs and base moldings than usual to give it an appropriately furniture look as well as to anchor it in the space.

The furniture look extends into the toekick detail on the sink wall. There was a practical purpose for this: The floor was off by almost a full inch from one end to the other (an old house fact of life). The decorative toekick and moldings along the bottom helped camouflage the flaw.

Teacup knobs in the breakfast bar lighten the space with charm and whimsy while sharing a finish with the more traditional hardware throughout the rest of the kitchen and butler's pantry.

above • This spacious kitchen and butler's pantry exudes Southern hospitality, fitting for a former boarding house known across the region for its family-style Sunday dinners.

right • The schoolhouse style pendant over the sink adds both coordinating style and task lighting in this key location.

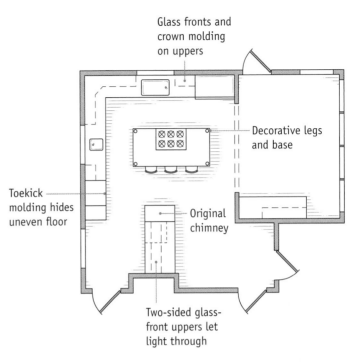

Glass fronts and
crown molding
on uppers

Decorative legs
and base

Toekick
molding hides
uneven floor

Original
chimney

Two-sided glass-
front uppers let
light through

left • Double warming
drawers keep food at
the right temperature
for late-arriving
party-goers and family
members on separate
schedules.

right • The pro-style gas
range top is enhanced
by a deck-mounted pot
filler for conveniently
filling large pots.

APPLIANCES

Appliances are the engine of your kitchen, performing the vital tasks of moving dinner from cold storage to hot stove to clean spoon. Today, appliances are being asked to do ever more in new and innovative ways.

From Basic to Multitasking

Many kitchen remodels begin because of one failing appliance. Its breakdown signals an opportunity for improvements not just in basic performance, but potentially also in energy and water savings, new functions, and added style.

There are entirely new categories of appliances—residential warming drawers, built-in coffee systems, and speed-cook ovens—that may not have existed when your home was built. And there are also new configurations, like microwave drawers and refrigerator columns, in now-standard appliances that offer unprecedented flexibility in redesigning your kitchen. No longer locked into traditional shapes or sizes, today's appliance offerings take you far beyond the Model T options of yesteryear and add massive horsepower to your design plan.

One of the most recent and popular refrigerator configurations is the French door. Available in standard depth, countertop depth, and built-in models, this configuration offers ultra-wide shelves suitable for catering trays and pizza boxes.

"Hiding" Appliances

The trend toward open-floor-plan homes is driving a related trend toward minimizing appliances. When the kitchen is completely open to neighboring gathering spaces, many homeowners want the mechanics and mess of the kitchen to disappear.

This accounts for the increased popularity of integrated dishwashers, warming drawers, and refrigerators. It also accounts for cooking ventilation that hides within cabinetry and glass-fronted appliances that camouflage their power.

All of these appliance offerings, along with related advances in cabinetry and fixtures, seek to create a hidden or "un"-kitchen look that offers new possibilities in high-end design. This is especially prevalent in contemporary, European-inspired spaces.

above • Matching cabinetry panels are being used for hiding beverage refrigerators, whether they're door or drawer models.

above • Ventilation inserts and ducting are often hidden behind matching or coordinating cabinetry elements, especially in traditional kitchens.

above • Hiding appliances behind panels is popular in modern kitchens, as well as in traditional ones. It's even possible to have continuous integrated handles across a cabinet run that includes a dishwasher for nonstop sleek style.

Updating Appliances in Existing Kitchens

It's not uncommon to find kitchens with fabulous old cabinets and countertops but not-so-fabulous old appliances. Even if they're in working condition, chances are they're less energy efficient than today's models and offer fewer features than you may want.

Some appliances are easy to replace. A standard 30-inch range will fit into the same space as an older range of the same size. So will a newer, water-saving, Energy Star®–rated 24-inch dishwasher. Even a new over-the-range microwave will likely fit into the same opening as an older model, but the new version may have more cooking features to offer. It's likely, too, that you'll be able to find a new freestanding counter-depth refrigerator that fits into your existing opening, as there are so many sizes on the market today.

Where appliance replacement becomes a bit more challenging is fitting new built-in appliances into existing cut-outs. It may be doable, but you will need to be certain of the height, width, and depth measurements so that what you're buying will fit into your cabinetry. As most older American cabinetry is face-frame based, unless you know which company made them and can get related specifications, you have no way of knowing the weight or cut-out tolerances allowed by the manufacturer to maintain the structural integrity of the cabinet. This is where it will be worth your time and expense to consult with a professional.

I don't recommend trying to buy panel-ready appliances to fit into existing cabinetry unless you're also refinishing or refacing. The two will be nearly impossible to match otherwise.

With additional settings like speed cook, convection, and warming, an over-the-range microwave can effectively turn one convenience appliance into many.

Unlike their gas and electric cousins, an induction range delivers professional-caliber cooking performance with superior energy savings. Convection and a second oven deliver even more cooking capabilities and a warming feature.

A new dishwasher can save on water and energy use, as well as offering quiet operation and additional cleaning modes like sanitizing and crystal.

New appliances can convert this charming budget kitchen into a high performer without replacing any cabinetry, flooring, backsplash, or countertop.

A new countertop-depth refrigerator brings sleeker style, new energy savings, and more specialized cooling options for wine, produce, and other fresh foods.

Freestanding or Designer Types

One of the first decisions you'll make when incorporating new appliances into a kitchen remodel is whether to have them be freestanding or built-in. Built-in appliances are commonly found in upscale kitchen projects, as they provide a more streamlined look. Built-in refrigerators, freezers, dishwashers, and warming drawers can be paneled to match the surrounding cabinetry for an integrated look. Built-in ovens and microwaves now offer sleeker frames that extend minimally, or not at all, from their cabinetry cut-outs. The cost for these design enhancements is significant; it's not unusual for a premium appliance package like this to cost three to four times what you'd pay for a standard suite. I suggest them for kitchens in luxury neighborhoods where they're expected.

An alternative to a built-in refrigerator is a freestanding countertop-depth model. It will fit into most existing openings, but only the doors and handles will extend beyond the cabinet faces. This type of refrigerator is easy to plan into an appliance upgrade or kitchen remodel. Planning for the cabinetry to be "boxed" rather than built in gives a richer look than a standard-depth refrigerator, which can extend intrusively into the kitchen. You can also recess a wall space to give a standard refrigerator a cabinet-depth look from the front. This is an especially good option if you don't want to lose the typical 4- to 5-cubic-foot capacity difference between countertop depth and standard depth or if you want to reuse an existing refrigerator.

In ranges, you also have a freestanding or premium choice, a slide-in range. The traditional 30-inch range with controls in a raised back panel is considered freestanding. This has a style and functional disadvantage: The raised back interferes with backsplash design and the controls end up behind pots, making them harder to see and reach. Slide-in ranges have their controls up front, where they are more accessible. They also offer more streamlined style. Not surprisingly, there is a cost premium; a slide-in range with the same features as a freestanding model can cost almost twice as much.

A style-friendly alternative to a costly built-in refrigerator is a countertop-depth model.

left · Built-in refrigerators cost thousands more than freestanding models but impart luxurious style to a kitchen, especially when clad in matching cabinetry panels and hardware.

above · Most professionally designed remodels with 30-inch ranges include slide-in styles rather than freestanding versions. The backless slide-ins allow for better backsplash visibility.

right · More-affordable slide-in ranges offer the convenience of front-mounted controls that avoid reaching past hot pots to change the setting.

Range or Cooktop and Ovens

It is now possible for even a dedicated chef to get great cooking performance from either a range or a cooktop and ovens. The primary factors in choosing one configuration versus the other are space, accessibility, and style.

SPACE

Space-wise, it's far easier to fit a standard 30-inch or even a pro-style 36-inch range into a small kitchen than it is to make space for both a 30-inch cooktop and 30-inch double ovens. A 30-inch or 36-inch range, which combines a cooking surface and single or double ovens, can offer some of the same dual fuel, convection, and warming features as separate ovens. Its main virtues are space-saving performance and a single price tag. These virtues fade when you start considering 48-inch or 60-inch models. The latter will command the same space as a standard cooktop and wall ovens. They will also eat up a larger portion of your kitchen investment.

ACCESSIBILITY

Another factor in choosing range or cooktop and ovens is accessibility. Some homeowners—especially seniors—lack the flexibility or upper body strength to pull a large entrée out of a range cavity. It's set so low to the floor that bending down to lift a heavy roast or turkey becomes a daunting challenge. Mounting double ovens side by side at a comfortable height can offset these physical limitations.

A standard counter-height-mounted cooktop will work for many users. For those with mobility challenges, the cooktop can be mounted at a lower table height for easier wheelchair or seated use. A range top that offers controls on a front panel (like a pro-style range), rather than a standard cooktop with top-set controls, would be an additional convenience for mobility-challenged users.

facing page top · A pro-style range with double ovens is another approach to gaining high performance and increased cooking capability.

facing page bottom · Induction is the newest entry in the performance cooktop category and is favored by professional chefs across Europe for its superior temperature control, speed, and energy efficiency.

left · Double ovens are often a cooking enthusiast's first choice, as they offer multiple settings and large capacity for regular entertaining.

STYLE

A final consideration for range versus cooktop and ovens is style. If you're after the European-inspired hidden-kitchen look, then a sleek induction cooktop with ovens hiding behind sliding cabinet doors will fit the look much better than a range, whatever its size. For a traditional or transitional kitchen, a cooktop and wall oven are considered by some to be a premium design feature, but this is mainly in comparison to a typical 30-inch freestanding range with one oven cavity. Larger, feature-rich ranges have made this preference somewhat outdated; today, you have more flexibility than ever in finding the cooking solution that works best for you.

Ultimately, your choice of cooktop and oven versus range will be primarily determined by your physical limitations as well as the limitations of your kitchen. Price and style factor in, too. Happily, there are high-performance options in both choices.

The sleek lines of induction cooktops make them a perfect choice for modern kitchen designs. Their energy savings and easy cleanability are also ideal for modern living.

Continuous grates over the burners make sliding a heavy pot or pan away from the flame easier for the home chef.

Dual-Fuel Ranges

Many electric range owners crave the chef-level performance of a gas cooktop. Many gas range owners—especially those who enjoy baking—dislike the uneven cooking performance of their gas oven. A dual-fuel range with gas cooktop and electric oven could be the solution for both, especially one with a convection feature. Convection makes cooking and baking faster, less drying, and more even.

The disadvantages of dual-fuel ranges are their higher cost to purchase and install relative to a standard range and the limited selection in a 30-inch size for those who just want to replace one appliance, rather than remodel their kitchen. In addition, if you don't currently have access to gas in your community, you'll have to arrange for an alternative source and installation, adding to the cost of this purchase.

Many designer kitchens feature chunky range tops with front controls. Given their unique shape and installation requirements, they are typically added into a full kitchen remodel rather than as a single appliance replacement.

Cooking Ventilation

Cooking ventilation is crucial for your health, safety, and the overall comfort of your home. It pulls odors, grease, and gasses out of your kitchen and house through properly connected ducts. Ducting outside from a wall-, cabinet-, or ceiling-mounted ventilation unit over the cooking surface is the ideal scenario, but isn't always possible in condo projects or more affordable remodels.

Some island or peninsula cooktop installations are paired with downdraft ventilation. If the kitchen sits over a crawlspace or basement rather than the commonly found concrete slab foundation, these may also be ducted outside. In general, though, downdraft vents are less efficient than overhead options.

For those situations when you absolutely can't vent outside, a recirculation kit in a downdraft system, vent hood, or over-the-range microwave may be the only substitute. These kits pull the cooking steam, gasses, and grease through a filter, clean it somewhat, and send it back into the kitchen.

Given the importance of including cooking ventilation in your kitchen plan, it's no surprise that it has evolved into a crucial style choice, as well as a performance component. Some design plans call for hidden ventilation. This could take the shape of a downdraft model retracting into the countertop or a wall-mounted insert hiding behind millwork, stonework, or even inside a cabinet.

Other plans use a decorative vent hood as a design focal point. There is a wide range of styles and materials available to create your look. Contemporary kitchens may call on sleek steel and glass, whereas traditional spaces could opt for hammered copper or a custom-painted hood to match a vintage-style range.

Whichever design direction you go, it's important to choose an insert or hood that meets the size and ventilation specifications for your cooking surface and that conforms to local building codes. Most important is that you actually use it while you're cooking. (Choose the quietest model you can afford, so that you're not tempted to leave it off or have to shout over it.)

above • Ventilation can be hidden behind matching cabinetry elements and still do its job effectively.

above • Downdraft ventilation is popular for island cooking to maintain sight lines around the room, but it needs to be exceptionally powerful to do its job as well as an overhead model.

top • A professional-style stainless hood will always pair well with a pro-style stainless range.

above • Many kitchens are designed for under-cabinet vent hoods. Their ductwork runs through the storage above and through the wall or ceiling beyond, unless they're equipped with a recirculating kit.

left • Island hoods offer better ventilation capacity than downdraft vents. They should be one size larger than the cooktop to better capture escaping steam, smoke, and gasses.

Cooking Tools

RANGES
$ to $$$

- Combine a cooking surface and one or more ovens into a single 24-inch or larger appliance with four to eight burners and accessories. The most common size is 30 inches.

- Cooking surface can be gas, electric, or induction, and ovens can be gas or electric. Dual-fuel models include gas cooktops and electric ovens.

- Cooktop accessories for 36-inch and larger ranges can include grills, griddles, or wok burners.

- Ranges may include double ovens, convection ovens, or warming drawers, even in standard 30-inch models.

- Ranges are typically offered in freestanding models with the controls on a raised panel behind the burners or in slide-in versions with controls in the front and no raised back panel.

- Stainless steel has been the leading luxury finish for many years, but is about to be joined in that category by glass-front appliances, especially smartphone-inspired white and black versions.

COOKTOPS
$ to $$$

- Cooktops can sit directly on the countertop with top-mounted controls or, in a range-top configuration, extend into the cabinetry front below with front-mounted controls.

- Like the burners on a range, these units can be gas, electric, or induction. There are also modular units that allow you to combine cooking types by pairing different burner modules.

- Most common sizes for electric and induction cooktops are 30 inch and 36 inch. Gas is the most popular option for the larger 48-inch and 60-inch models.

- Grills, griddles, and woks are popular cooktop add-on features.

- Induction cooktops are the most energy-efficient and easiest to clean.

WALL OVENS
$$ to $$$

- Wall ovens come in single or double models. Singles are often mounted below a cooktop.

- Combination wall ovens pair a standard or convection oven with a convection microwave oven for added functionality.

- Although called wall ovens, singles often mount in a base cabinet, whereas doubles usually mount in tall cabinets.

- Convection and speed-cooking features are increasingly popular in wall ovens. Some models may also include a pizza mode designed to produce the extra heat associated with brick ovens or steam for healthy cooking and reheating.

MICROWAVES AND STEAM COOKERS
$ to $$$

- Microwave ovens are available in countertop models, built-in models with trim kits, over-the-range models with vent fans, and drawer models that mount below countertops.

- Many microwaves today offer such multitasking functions as speed-cook, convection, and warming capabilities.

- Steam cookers perform most of the same defrosting, speed cooking, and reheating functions as microwaves, with the exception of making microwave popcorn. They may be mounted in cabinetry like ovens or installed in countertops. They may be connected to the home's plumbing lines or function independently with built-in reservoirs.

Professional-style ranges with double ovens are a popular choice for large, upscale kitchens. Their cost, performance, and size preclude their use in every home.

above • Microwave ovens are available in different sizes and configurations to meet a wide range of kitchen designs.

above • The controls on some induction cooktops illuminate when in use and go dark for a sleeker look when not being used.

Refrigerators and Freezers

Most American homes of the past 40 years have had a combination refrigerator and freezer that met the household's food-preservation needs. Over time, manufacturers offered choices in top-mount or bottom-mount freezers or side-by-side combinations. Ice and water dispensers on these side-by-side models gained popularity for the convenience they offered.

Later came the French-door models with double refrigerator doors above and a single or double freezer drawer below. Refrigerator drawers that install below countertops as supplemental appliances also came on the market and greatly assist in the creation of zoned kitchen plans.

Refrigerators and freezers now come in independent columns, too, that can be installed side by side or in completely separate locations in the kitchen. These all-refrigerator and all-freezer configurations give the designer and homeowner more flexibility in food storage and placement.

top • Undercounter refrigerator drawers, available in panel-ready or stainless-steel options, give you more flexibility in zoning your kitchen design.

right • Built-in refrigerators clad in matching cabinetry panels and hardware are an ideal choice for upscale traditional kitchens.

Built-in refrigerators are available in stainless steel, and the most popular configurations include side by side, French door, and standard bottom freezer.

A countertop-depth freestanding refrigerator can be boxed in with panels and cabinetry to give it an upscale built-in look at a fraction of the built-in price.

Cooling Tools

REFRIGERATOR–FREEZER COMBINATIONS
$ to $$$

- Most popular home refrigeration purchase, typically in 33-inch or 36-inch widths for full-size models.
- Available as built-in or freestanding units.
- Freestanding units may be standard depth (typically between 31 inches and 34 inches with handles) or reduced countertop depth, where only the doors and handles extend past the 24-inch-deep cabinet fronts.
- Built-in models are available in popular finishes or panel-ready for cabinet-matching fronts.
- Popular configurations include top-mount freezer, bottom-mount freezer, side by side, and French door with single or double drawers.
- Popular options include specialty drawers, gallon-size door bins, ice and water dispensers, and frost-free freezers.

REFRIGERATOR AND FREEZER COLUMNS
$$$

- All-refrigerator and all-freezer models are available for use next to each other or in separate locations. These upscale, built-in offerings allow for size customization according to a homeowner's food-storage and space needs.
- Sizes range from 18 inches to 36 inches in width, with European manufacturers typically offering the narrower sizes.
- Wine storage is a popular refrigerator column option.

REFRIGERATOR AND FREEZER DRAWERS
$$ to $$$

- Refrigerator drawers have become increasingly popular as supplemental, point-of-use cold-food storage on islands.
- Typically 24 inches wide with two separate cold food-storage drawers.
- Available in popular finishes or panel-ready.

WINE AND BEVERAGE REFRIGERATION
$ to $$$

- Wine refrigeration has become popular for climate-controlled storage of a homeowners' collection.
- Available in full-height and undercounter configurations and in varied widths from 15 inches, 18 inches, or 24 inches for undercounter models to 30 inches for full-height columns.
- Also available in single-zone or dual-zone for preservation of white and red wines.
- Beverage refrigerators are similar in size and placement but offer a more family-friendly option.

above • Compact kitchens call for compact refrigerators. European manufacturers tend to offer the widest selection in style and energy efficiency.

facing page top right • Hiding a built-in refrigerator behind matching cabinetry panels is a design strategy for minimizing its hefty bulk.

facing page top left • Including a wine refrigerator in your kitchen is an ideal way to store this popular dinner or party accompaniment. Dual-zone models are best for red and white collections.

facing page bottom • Refrigerator and freezer-only columns in varying widths add tremendous design flexibility to a new kitchen.

Dishwashers

Like so many other appliance categories, dishwashers have evolved from 1960s-era rolling models that attached to the kitchen faucet to the feature-loaded, energy-efficient, water-saving household essentials they are today.

Even more affordable models on the market now often have pot-scrubber and china/crystal settings to meet a wider range of cleaning needs. Though typically 24 inches wide, there are 18-inch models available for homes wanting a secondary dishwasher, increasingly popular in upscale kitchens or in those where home cooks entertain a lot.

Dishwashers are available in popular finishes or panel-ready for matching cabinet fronts. They are also available in standard single-compartment or dual-drawer configurations. Drawer dishwashers are ideal for smaller households that can benefit from smaller-load washing and for separating loads, such as into fragile and bulky for dinner-party hosts or meat and dairy dishes for kosher households.

Popular dishwasher options include timer operation that lets you schedule a load when the household is asleep or during off-peak energy hours, flexible racking systems to accommodate different loads, and integrated consoles that aren't seen from the machine's exterior.

In addition to cleaning performance, dishwashers can be selected according to their Energy Star rating for electrical use, manufacturer-supplied water-saving information, and decibel levels. The lower the number, the quieter the dishwasher and the easier it is to hold a conversation in the kitchen while it's running. They range from the low 40s for machines it's hard to hear running when standing next to them to the high 60s for dishwashers that will interfere with TV watching in the open-plan family room dozens of feet away.

above • Dishwasher drawers are ideal for those who run small loads or want to separate dishes for religious purposes.

left • A dishwasher doesn't need to be seen (or heard) to do its job well. Panel-ready models with ultra-quiet operation are widely available today.

One family-friendly dishwasher innovation is hidden controls (on the top of the door) that keep young children from starting or stopping a cycle without adult supervision.

The Extras

A wide range of appliances have joined the standards for cooking, cleanup, and food preservation. You always want to factor in all of the appliances you'll be purchasing for your kitchen in advance, not just the large ones. That way, their size, location, electrical load and switching needs, plumbing considerations, and door swings, where applicable, can be factored into your kitchen plan. Here are some appliances you may want to consider in your remodeled kitchen.

BUILT-IN COFFEE SYSTEMS

Coffee systems offer an upscale alternative to the countertop machine, but at a much higher price tag. For connoisseurs who crave instant gratification and clutter-free counters, this may be a desired luxury. Some models come with plumbing hook-ups. Others rely on reservoir systems.

WARMING DRAWERS

If your household members are all on different schedules and your range or microwave oven doesn't have a warming feature, this could be a very helpful appliance to plan into your kitchen project. Warming drawers come in popular finishes or panel-ready models to match your cabinets. Typically, they're installed below wall ovens, but they can be placed below a countertop for greater convenience, as long as there is electrical power available at that location.

top • A warming drawer is the ultimate kitchen extra for those households that entertain regularly or just keep widely different schedules.

right • True coffee enthusiasts will enjoy the high-end style and convenience of a built-in coffee system; beware, though, as these systems are pricey.

ICE MAKERS

These are ideal for households that love entertaining large groups. Ice makers will require both electrical and water supply to do their job but can be an ideal supplement to freezers without one or for those homeowners who need more ice on a regular basis than standard ice makers will produce.

TRASH COMPACTORS

Reduce your trips to the curbside trash bin and the volume you send to landfills by installing a trash compactor. These will fit into the space you might otherwise plan for a pull-out trash can in your kitchen, but you'll still want a separate recycling bin. Trash compactors are a requirement in some communities with stringent waste regulations.

above · Some communities require a trash compactor to reduce landfill demands. Your household might enjoy the reduced trips to the curb on trash day, too.

right · Ice makers are ideal appliances for homeowners who entertain large groups on a regular basis.

The New Multitaskers

After decades of size inflation, homes have started to return to more manageable proportions. This means fewer McMansion kitchens and more realistically scaled spaces. Although this also means less square footage available for appliances, it does not mean a sacrifice in performance. The latest trend is the multi-tasker—a single appliance that serves multiple roles.

One of the original examples of this trend was the microwave that doubled as a convection oven. This meant that kitchens too small for a cooktop and double ovens could have a second oven by using the microwave's convection setting. Newer microwaves also include steam, speed-cook, or warmer features, delivering three or four appliances in the space of one.

Steam cooking and warming drawers also have shown up in ranges, adding versatility and increased performance to those kitchen staples, too.

Multitasking is available in refrigeration, as well, with drawer-based and standard-height models providing convertible fridge–freezer–wine storage options. These offerings allow you to switch from one setting to another and back—an ideal convenience when entertaining.

above · Sometimes you need extra refrigerator space, and other times you need extra freezer capacity. From time to time, you might want a wine cooler, too. The new multitaskers offer that flexibility in one appliance.

left · Microwave ovens, even countertop models, now commonly multitask. Added functions include speed-cook, convection, and steam cooking.

above · Fridge–freezer–wine storage multitasking even comes in under-counter configuration for the ultimate in zoned kitchen versatility.

above · Many space-challenged kitchens are limited to over-the-range microwave placement. Multitasking models that also speed-cook, warm, and convection-bake put three or four appliances in the compact space of one.

above · Ranges multitask now, too. The latest incorporate convection, warming, grilling, and even steaming.

Entertainment and Information in the Kitchen

You may not consider televisions, computers, or tablets to be kitchen appliances, but many homes now incorporate entertainment and data into their regular kitchen functions, and these need to be planned for just as your traditional appliances do. If you're integrating technology into your kitchen remodel, you or your designer will likely partner with an electronics professional.

TELEVISIONS

Televisions aren't terribly new to kitchens—they've just gotten larger, more sophisticated, and more technology driven. Some double as computer screens, and because they almost all require a cable box or satellite dish, their place in the kitchen can be limited.

Their wiring, safe operation, sight lines, and input source—be it cable, cellular, wireless Internet access, or emerging technology—all need to be factored into your kitchen planning. Because the TV and its related source box might both be large, you're going to have to decide where they will least impact precious kitchen storage space while still serving your viewing preferences. If a remote location is available for the source box, that's ideal, but its connection to the television will still need to be managed in the planning and installation process.

above • It's not unusual to find laptops and tablets being used in the kitchen today. It's crucial to find a spot away from heat and water with a power connection for their regular use.

right • Televisions are increasingly finding their way into kitchens as entertainment appliances. Finding space for them and their connection requirements often demands professionals with specialized skill.

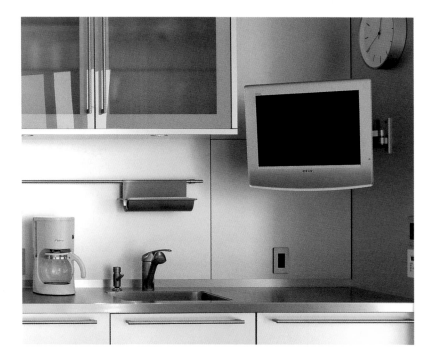

above • Pivoting mounting arms allow wall-mounted televisions to be seen from multiple locations in the kitchen.

below • Sturdy new lift mechanisms allow a television to be hidden below a countertop when it's not being used.

If you want to incorporate a television for viewing while working or eating, it's crucial to plan a location and mounting system that lets you see it from your preferred vantage points. You might want to tie it to a keyboard or tablet to take advantage of Internet functionality. Those details will require careful planning, as well, to ensure that everything works and that delicate components aren't in the way of potentially damaging kitchen chores.

TABLETS

Just as dishwashers and microwaves slowly proved their convenience to the mid-century homemaker and became the essential kitchen appliances they are today, tablets are moving in that direction, as well. Home-automation specialists are tying basic home functions like lights, climate, security, and entertainment to new tablet apps and building them into walls and countertops. Some technology companies predict that your entire countertop will become a data center in future years, giving you access to recipes, cooking hotlines, cleaning tips, and other kitchen-friendly Internet offerings.

If you want to incorporate a tablet into your kitchen, plan for your Internet source—most likely a whole-house wireless system—and a dry, protected spot with a charging port where you'll use it most.

above • The popularity of MP3 players and smartphones has created new charging and storage challenges for kitchens. A countertop hideaway system is one innovative solution.

The Well-Equipped Kitchen

This modern waterfront Pensacola, Florida, home was built around the kitchen design plan for a homeowner who loves to cook and entertain. She wanted a cozy environment where friends could enjoy a glass of wine from the peninsula wine captain while she whips up dinner.

The professional refrigerator was a must, and the rest of the kitchen was built around it. The enthusiastic home chef also wanted refrigerator drawers on her island to keep prep foods in reach of the range top and prep sink. This layout lets her access the burners and fresh foods while chatting with her guests.

The challenge in this new construction project was to have a good amount of professional cooking equipment—including extras like a steam oven and built-in coffee system—and a traffic flow that didn't interfere with meal preparation. As large windows were prioritized over wall cabinets, a unique pantry/prep kitchen with supplemental tall and island storage was sited next to the main "entertaining" kitchen. This area also houses a prep sink, extra oven, and icemaker. Traffic flow is optimized around the pantry appliances, too, with sliding rather than swinging cabinet doors.

Although loaded with top-of-the-line appliances and chef add-ons, the kitchen still feels homey and blends brightly with its casual surroundings.

top · **This large, pro-style refrigerator was on the homeowner's must-have list. Its four drawers and glass front mean quick access to all of its contents during busy meal and party prep sessions.**

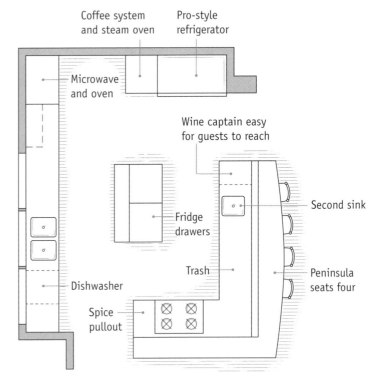

Coffee system and steam oven

Pro-style refrigerator

Microwave and oven

Wine captain easy for guests to reach

Fridge drawers

Second sink

Trash

Peninsula seats four

Dishwasher

Spice pullout

This incredibly well-equipped kitchen was designed for regular cooking and entertaining, keeping guests close to the host but out of the work flow.

above • This handsome copper farmhouse-style sink adds both functionality and flair to the elegant cook's kitchen.

above • The professional-style range top faces guests at both bar and table, but its large, powerful island hood ensures that the kitchen stays comfortable for all, even when all of the burners are engaged.

COUNTERTOPS

Countertops are the handsome,

unsung heroes of your kitchen,

AND

providing an essential work surface

for all kinds of tasks.

BACKSPLASHES

Countertop Materials

While doing their job efficiently, countertops also add a strong visual element to your kitchen, so the material you choose should take both practicality and style into account. There is a growing selection from which to choose, including economical (and increasingly attractive) laminates, affordable tile and new European-import ceramic and porcelain slab alternatives, easy-maintenance Corian and its many solid-surface competitors, natural and engineered stone, glass, concrete, stainless steel, bamboo, and even recycled paper.

It's not uncommon for a larger kitchen to combine two materials, one as a practical work surface, the other as a pretty focal point.

When choosing your countertops, consider how you will use them—and where, if you're combining materials. Will this be a baking center, where you might want the coolness of stone? What material will coordinate well with that stone's color and possible pattern? What's left in the budget for the other tops, and can those be installed by the same fabricator?

Consider, too, your new top's upkeep. You might love the idea of a butcher block prep counter, but you have to be willing to oil it on a regular basis. A Calcutta marble counter in a magazine can easily seduce with its creamy glow, but think about whether you will love it when it's stained and worn after many years of use. Countertops are a financial investment, so your decisions should all be long-term focused.

top left • Granite and engineered stone countertops typically feature undermount sinks, an easy-maintenance look.

left • Engineered stone counters, also called quartz, offer the heat and scratch resistance of granite but come with a warranty and never need to be sealed.

above • Waterfall ends are a very popular, durable, and stylish way to complete a modern stone-countertop installation.

Countertops

LAMINATE
$

- Most affordable countertop option to buy and install.
- Simple layouts lend themselves to do-it-yourself installation.
- Widely available in most areas; often in stock at home centers for the lowest cost.
- Work best with a drop-in sink rather than an undermounted model.
- Often easy to damage.
- Generally not repairable.

SOLID SURFACE
$$

- Large selection of colors and patterns available.
- Nearly seamless in their appearance.
- Most lines offer integral sinks and a seamless coved backsplash for clean style and easy cleanup.
- Require no sealing.
- Repairable.

NATURAL STONE
$$ to $$$$

- Most often granite or marble slab, but soapstone is also included in this class.
- Granite can be polished to a reflective sheen or honed or flamed for a matte look.
- Polished granite has become more cost-effective as it has grown in popularity.
- Natural veining, pattern, and irregularities are part of their natural appeal.
- Natural stone needs to be periodically sealed.
- Granite is extremely scratch- and heat-resistant but can be scorched and dull your knives; cutting boards and trivets are recommended.
- Marble is a soft stone, prone to chipping and staining.
- Typically installed with an undermount or farmhouse sink.

Both natural and engineered stone countertops come with polished (seen here) or matte finishes for completely different looks.

STAINLESS STEEL
$$$

- Hygienic and easy to clean, but it will show streaks, fingerprints, and water spots.
- Often paired with an integral sink.
- Good heat resistance.
- Readily shows easy-to-acquire scratches and dents.
- Can be noisy.

ENGINEERED STONE/QUARTZ
$$$

- Offer comparable heat and scratch resistance to granite.
- Typically installed with an undermount or farmhouse sink, but some brands now offer an integral-style sink.
- Nonporous, so they never needs to be sealed.
- Available in solid colors and patterns seeking to mimic natural stone.
- Available in polished or matte finishes.
- Typically include a 10-year or longer warranty against defects.

above • A plank-style wood countertop offers warmth and elegance to a room, but most come with maintenance requirements that should be considered before purchasing one.

above • Newer engineered stone counters better imitate natural stone while offering superior stain resistance.

WOOD AND BAMBOO
$$$

- Warm, elegant finishes like teak or cherry planks or more workaday maple or oak butcher block available.
- Needs to be sealed against moisture.
- These higher-end materials are often used for focal points like islands or bar tops rather than throughout the kitchen.
- Can be sanded for scratch and stain removal.
- Eco-friendly alternatives, like reclaimed lumber and sustainably harvested species, are available.
- Though technically a fast-growing, sustainable grass, not a tree, bamboo is often grouped in the wood category for its similar properties.

CONCRETE
$ to $$$

- Offers extraordinary customizability in color, pattern, insets, and shapes.
- Can be an affordable do-it-yourself project with careful research.
- Poured-in-place concrete ideal for seamless appearance in oversize spaces or those interrupted by posts.
- Can accept an integral sink.
- Can crack and stain.
- Need to be sealed to protect finish.
- Some concrete tops—particularly thicker installations—require extra support; if you're creating them yourself, be sure to research this for your project.

GLASS
$$$

- Glass tops fall into two general categories: recycled blend and solid slab.
- Blended tops combine glass shards from recycled materials with a cement binder for a smooth, colorful, polished surface.
- The cement mix makes the blended tops porous and sealing is recommended.
- Slab tops are nonporous and never need to be sealed.
- Slab glass comes in a textured, translucent finish that is ideal for underlighting.
- Recycled blend and slab are both considered sustainable.

CERAMIC AND PORCELAIN SLAB
$$$

- European innovation just starting to be imported into the North American market.
- Extremely stain-, heat-, and scratch-resistant, like their tile counterparts.
- Much thinner and lighter than stone, with comparable durability.
- Can be installed over other countertops for reduced replacement cost.
- Most often shown with an undermount sink, but integral sinks are available, too.
- Initial limitation includes 48-inch width maximum; this won't work for all islands.

STONE

In recent years, granite and engineered stone, which is also referred to as quartz, have dominated kitchen countertop trends. Granite, of course, has been with us for millennia. It's valued for its durable heat- and scratch-resistant surface and prized for its natural beauty. The fact that it's porous means it can absorb bacteria, and it needs to be kept sealed against staining.

Marble is another popular, elegant stone for kitchen countertops, but it's much softer than granite and even more stain-prone. Limestone and soapstone are sometimes specified for kitchens. Both are also porous materials with natural beauty that require sealing maintenance.

Engineered stone or quartz countertops have grown popular because they're heat- and scratch-resistant like granite, but nonporous, less prone to staining, and maintenance-free. They are typically made of 90 percent quartz and compressed with binders and pigment to give them their strength and appearance.

Quartz tops are sold under the Silestone®, Cambria®, Zodiaq®, Caesarstone®, and other brand names; some have recycled content and sustainability benefits. They are available in monochromatic tones or patterns that mimic granite or marble. Because they are an engineered material, they typically lack the naturalistic variations of those surfaces. This is most obvious in a side-by-side comparison. However, as quartz manufacturers rapidly improve their design techniques, their products' lack of natural variation is becoming less obvious every year.

In general, suppliers of quartz tops offer a 10-year or longer warranty, which has also increased their market share. Like other stone tops, engineered versions are typically installed with undermount or farmhouse sinks for the most upscale look and easiest maintenance. Some suppliers are starting to offer integral sinks in the same material, though most often in select neutrals rather than in a color or pattern that matches the top.

above • Farmhouse and undermount sinks both require that the stone top's exposed edge surrounding them be completely finished.

above • No two slabs of granite are identical. Each has its own unique patterns, color combinations, and natural beauty marks.

above • Marble countertops are prized for their natural beauty and cool surface but are very stain prone. It's now possible to get a comparable look from engineered stone with stain resistance and greater durability.

far left • Engineered stone offers a flawlessly smooth, nonporous surface that's easy to maintain—and perfect for rolling dough.

left • Stone countertops can be edged in different ways to yield different styles. The eased edge shown here works perfectly in transitional kitchens.

SOLID SURFACE

Another popular countertop material is solid surface, though it has lost some of its upscale luster to stone. These acrylic or polyester with resin tops are most frequently referred to as Corian, one of the most popular brand names.

Unlike quartz or granite, solid-surface tops are not cold and hard to the touch. They also offer a uniquely seamless appearance, especially when installed with an integral sink and coved backsplash. This gives them a sleek appearance and makes them easier to maintain, as there are fewer crevices to catch kitchen grime. Like quartz, they're nonporous, so sealing is not required.

Also like their quartz counterparts, solid-surface tops come in monochromatic or natural stone patterns. They, too, have improved their aesthetics over the years, but their soft, typical matte surface will rarely be mistaken for real stone.

Nonetheless, solid surface does have real benefits. One of its unique characteristics is repairability. You can sand out minor scratches (though consult with a pro before doing so), and more extensive damage can be repaired in your home by a professional. Done well, you'll never see where the damage had been.

Solid-surface countertops are an excellent choice for aging-in-place kitchens, as weaker vision is less likely to cause breakage when glasses are set down and a fall or bump against the softer solid-surface top can be less painful than one against stone. They also are a viable option for rental-property kitchens, given their repairability and low maintenance.

right • Solid-surface countertops are stain resistant and repairable, making them a family-friendly option.

above • Versatile solid surface can be installed with an apron-front sink and tile backsplash to create a more traditional look.

above • Solid-surface tops designed to look extra thick and modern use special installation techniques.

WOOD

Wood countertops are more often chosen for a select area of the kitchen rather than for the entire space due to cost, availability, and maintenance. These areas tend to fall into two main categories: a functional butcher block prep section or a decorative focal point. Many homeowners like butcher block's natural authenticity, rustic warmth, and cutting surface.

For practical applications, maple is the most common material for butcher block tops, given its hardness. Oak, walnut, and cherry are also options. Any wood species you choose needs to be regularly oiled and should be sealed in water-prone areas.

A focal-point wood countertop is most often selected for an island or bar top in a traditional or transitional kitchen, carefully chosen from matching planks for a glossy, seamless run with a thick, decorative edge. Walnut and cherry are popular options. Increasingly, you'll also find bamboo, Lyptus®, and reclaimed woods. Like their functional butcher block cousins, decorative wood tops should be kept as dry as possible and properly maintained.

right • This rustic black walnut top showcases the natural characteristics of wood, including its knots.

above • Butcher block countertops are prized as natural cutting and food preparation surfaces, but they do require regular sealing.

right • Like natural stone, no two wood tops are identical and many include beauty marks from their earlier life in the forest.

While traditional kitchens often feature focal-point wood tops, here a teak version coordinates stylishly with the modern space.

Mixing Countertop Materials for Form and Function

The kitchen in this nineteenth-century Park Slope (Brooklyn, New York) row house had butcher block tops that the homeowners loved when they purchased the home in the 1990s. They enjoyed the aesthetic warmth of the wood, as well as its natural cutting surface.

Unfortunately, the home suffered a major electrical fire in 2010 and the kitchen, along with much else in the house, had to be rebuilt. The owners wanted to keep as much of the original butcher block counters as could be salvaged. However, they had to change one key section so took savvy advantage of the opportunity forged by the fire and slightly relocated the sink.

They chose stainless steel for this countertop section for very functional reasons. First, it allowed for an integral sink, which would minimize teenager cleanup and splashing (which had been tough on the previous wood top). Second, it offered heat tolerance in case a pot had to be quickly moved off of the adjacent stove burners.

They still enjoy the warmth and natural beauty of their salvaged butcher block tops and matching new ones for the reconfigured and added sections of the kitchen. Only now they have the maintenance-free convenience of the stainless top and integral sink. To this Brooklyn family, that's the best of both worlds.

While they loved their butcher block countertops, the homeowners opted for stainless counters and an integral stainless sink in that corner for easier maintenance.

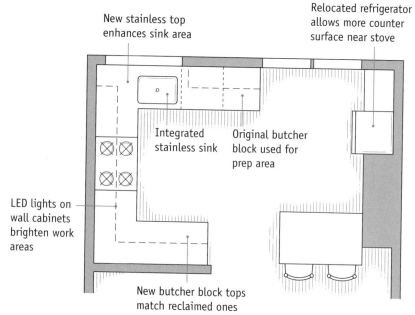

New stainless top enhances sink area

Relocated refrigerator allows more counter surface near stove

Integrated stainless sink

Original butcher block used for prep area

LED lights on wall cabinets brighten work areas

New butcher block tops match reclaimed ones

above • Pale green painted maple cabinets coordinate beautifully with the new wood floors that match the adjacent dining and living room's refinished planks, as well as with the kitchen's rescued butcher block counters.

left • Deep, wide pan drawers located near the range were part of the improvements designed into the new kitchen.

LAMINATE

High-pressure laminate countertops—often referred to generically as Formica® (even though that's a brand name)—are still a popular choice among affordable builders and remodelers. Manufacturers have improved their style in recent years, and they remain among the most budget-friendly countertop options, especially for kitchens that can take advantage of stock sizes available at home centers. (You can special-order an island or bar top in the same material for nonstock island and bar-top sizes and still enjoy tremendous savings.)

The drawbacks of laminate include a greater likelihood of damage from water penetrating their particleboard substrate around sinks, their lack of repairability if cut or chipped, and their budget-oriented perception for higher-end projects.

You have traditionally been limited to top-mounted sinks with laminate countertops, contributing to their lack of appeal for upscale remodelers. This is also slowly changing. New sink offerings and installation techniques now offer the opportunity to undermount a sink in a laminate top. You will want to be extra scrupulous in checking an installer's skill and credentials in this technique or risk the likelihood of ruining any tops (and possibly cabinets) in the vicinity of water.

Another positive attribute: Laminate-top installation and removal tend to be do-it-yourself friendly for a handy homeowner, which is not the case for solid surface or stone.

top right • Laminate has come a very long way in reproducing natural stone in an affordable, do-it-yourself friendly material.

right • Along with improved colors and patterns, laminate tops have improved their edge style offerings to more closely resemble the stone tops they're imitating.

above • The top choice of restaurateurs, stainless steel is a worry-free countertop surface for residential kitchens, too. Hot pots, messy spills, no problem!

above • Concrete tops can be poured in place for a seamless look at corners and around posts. They can also integrate seamless drain boards, trivet rod grooves, and decorative elements, if desired, for personalized style and functionality.

above • Concrete countertops offer tremendous design flexibility and do-it-yourself installation for the skilled amateur, but they are porous and require sealing.

STAINLESS STEEL

Most restaurant kitchens feature stainless-steel countertops because of their hygienic properties, heat resistance, and easy maintenance. In these utilitarian settings, noise, water spots, fingerprints, dents, and scratching are not a concern. They may be in your home, though. Over time, the top will take on a patina in which surface marks become part of its worn-in, pro-style appeal. If you're comfortable with this, you'll enjoy its hassle-free surface. You'll never have to seal it, oil it, worry about burning it with a hot pan, fret over spills staining your counter, or spend much time cleaning it. Many stainless-top owners also select an integral sink for additional convenience and sleek style.

CONCRETE

Concrete is one of the most versatile countertop materials available today. It can be blended with decorative elements like glass, fossils, or metal to create a custom design. It can be antiqued like an ancient floor or polished to a contemporary sheen. Concrete is ideal for kitchens with posts, unusual shapes, or counter runs longer than standard materials allow; your poured-in-place concrete counter will give you a seamless installation in all of these settings. It can also be combined with an integral sink, though not all local building codes allow it and you might not welcome the maintenance. In general, concrete counters are porous and need sealing. Although they are the only premium top that can be installed by capable do-it-yourselfers, concrete counters are highly dependent upon skilled installation and finishing to be properly supported, durable, sanitary, and usable for the rigors of kitchen life.

Matching New Countertops to Existing Flooring and Cabinets

Countertop replacements are among the most common kitchen updates today. Most often, you're swapping out laminate for more upscale alternatives like natural or engineered stone. Sometimes tile is being replaced due to the tiresome chore of grout cleanup. Whatever material you choose for your upgraded counters, it's crucial to select it in tandem with your lifestyle, cabinets, appliances, and flooring.

You'll want to choose a material that fits your lifestyle. Some require sealing, which you'll need to factor into your household maintenance. Others are prone to scratching or staining; review the information on pp. 114–115 for more details. Once you've selected the right surface—or surfaces—for your kitchen update, it's time to choose finishes that factor in the colors and patterns that won't be changed.

Busy woods like oak and cherry, either in your cabinets or flooring, work better with more monochromatic tops that won't create an overly busy look. Painted surfaces and a neutral floor tile can handle more pattern and pizzazz in the top. Be certain, though, when adding dramatic surfaces that you're confident you'll love them for as long as you plan to own your home and that they will appeal to future buyers if you plan on selling in the next few years.

A light-colored countertop will reflect more sunlight and ceiling light than a dark one, adding some brightness to your room. A dark top can add drama and a seamless look with black and stainless appliances. In general, the less contrast you introduce to a space, the larger it appears. If your kitchen is large and open, it can handle a bit more contrast than a small kitchen can.

If adjacent rooms open to the kitchen incorporate stone or tile—in a prominent fireplace surround or bar top, for instance—it's important to tie in those colors and patterns with your countertop choice or replace that material at the same time you're updating your kitchen so that the rooms share a similar aesthetic.

It's also important to factor related costs into your countertop replacement. In most instances you will also swap out the sink, faucet, and drains, adding to your material and labor budget. You will also probably be replacing the backsplash, both because it's likely to get damaged in the countertop-removal process and because it's probably of the same material you no longer want. Be sure to set aside funds for these not-insignificant add-ons.

This solid-surface top ties in the flooring, cabinet, and appliance colors of the kitchen shown at right, while offering a smooth, repairable, stain-resistant surface and integral sink potential.

THE EXISTING ROOM

While tile countertops offer durability and old world style, most homeowners dislike their grout staining and maintenance. New counters would greatly improve this kitchen's functionality and update its appearance.

Engineered stone countertops offer a heat-, scratch-, and stain-resistant surface. Its colors, too, coordinate with the cabinets, flooring, and countertops in the existing kitchen.

right • This brown porcelain slab countertop is also stain resistant and capable of holding an integral sink. It's as heat- and scratch-resistant as stone.

The New Countertop Materials: Ceramic and Porcelain Slab

When porcelain and ceramic are mentioned in connection with countertops, old-world tile and grout usually comes to mind. There's nothing old world about these new ceramic and porcelain slab tops emerging from Europe. And there's not a speck of grout—or grout upkeep—involved.

These new nonporous tops are as easy to maintain and are as heat- and scratch-resistant as granite and quartz plus they are far lighter and easier to install. They also take undermount sinks, like stone tops. Unlike stone, however, ceramic and porcelain slabs are primarily solid color with a matte finish and fine grain texture, though a few are emerging with stone-like patterns. The effect is crisp and natural at the same time. This manufactured material can also be made into integral sinks in the same color and texture as the countertop.

These tops tend to come in slabs the thickness of tile rather than the 2-cm or 3-cm thicknesses most often selected for American kitchens. They are built up on site with a matching edge, as are some stone installations. Early manufacturing technology also allows for a 4-foot width maximum, rendering them useless for over-size islands. Early edge styles are limited to eased and slightly mitered, so they're a fit mostly for contemporary and transitional kitchens wanting to merge clean style with cutting-edge technology.

Finally, early pricing puts them in the same range as engineered stone, but prices may fall as they gain acceptance and greater availability in North America. That may also result in manufacturing facilities being established on this side of the Atlantic.

above • Matte-textured countertops work especially well in modern kitchens; here, the countertop contrasts nicely with high-gloss finish cabinets and illuminated backsplashes.

above • These porcelain tops can be built up to whatever thickness is desired for style purposes or be laid thin over existing countertops.

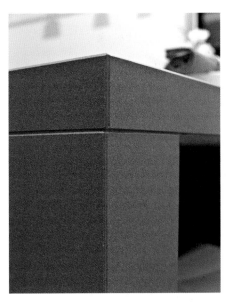

above • Countertops are fabricated from ultra-thin slabs of lightweight but ultra-strong porcelain or ceramic slab with mitered edges for a clean, contemporary look.

Backsplash Planning Considerations

A backsplash does more than just decorate the walls between your countertops and wall cabinets. Its noncombustible material protects the wall behind your cooking surface. It houses your electrical outlets for small appliances and switches for your garbage disposal and, possibly, undercabinet lighting. It can conceal wiring for that lighting, provide a design focal point for the kitchen, and hold organizing systems to free up counter and cabinet space.

Too often, a backsplash is a decorative afterthought. But given its multifaceted potential, careful planning should go into your kitchen's backsplash. Height and material are two of the considerations to keep in mind, but it's best to start with what you want the backsplash space to do. Ask yourself these questions to get started:

- Do you want to add outlets or switches? Where will they do the most good?

- Do you want to run some new lighting wire for undercabinet lights behind the backsplash?

- Will the backsplash be illuminated, requiring wiring of its own?

- Do you want to add any organizing systems to your backsplash space? If so, what types of organizers, how large, and how many? Where will the organizers be the most useful?

right • The focal-point design element here works because it's properly scaled and framed in its position.

Then consider the material and its installation:

- Will the backsplash be full height (to the wall cabinets or ceiling above) or a shorter height?

- Where will the backsplash start and end relative to windows and return walls, both vertically and horizontally?

- Will the backsplash be the same material as the countertops or something different? If different, will the additional material coordinate with the other surfaces in the space?

- If the backsplash is to include a focal-point element, have you ensured that an outlet, switch, or pot filler isn't planned for that specific location?

- Who will install the backsplash?

- Will a callback be required for the cabinet installers to add decorative elements and appliance garages after the backsplash material is installed?

top left · One of the key decisions in backsplash planning is where to end the material. In this installation, going all the way up the wall, rather than stopping at the wall cabinets, gives this section of the kitchen the same visual weight as the tall cabinets.

left · Full-height backsplashes create continuity between the countertop and the wall, but are typically higher-cost installations.

Backsplash Materials

The most common backsplash materials are tile and the material from which the countertop is made. Tile is one of the most versatile options, offering a wide array of colors, shapes, sizes, materials, styles, and even blends.

You are certainly not limited to these two options, however. Additional backsplash materials to consider include the following:

- **Tin tiles:** Real or imitation tin tiles come in a range of metallic and nonmetallic finishes. They can provide pattern as well as color. Many are easy to install yourself.

- **Wallpaper:** A scrubbable wallpaper can be an affordable, easy-to-live-with solution for your backsplash, especially if it ties in with paper installed in an adjacent space. Make sure local codes and the manufacturer's specifications allow for placement near a cooktop, or plan a different material or protective covering for that area.

- **Paint:** A decorative painter can create an original masterpiece on your backsplash and seal it to protect against cooking splashes.

- **Onyx and translucent engineered stone:** These luxurious options bring elegance and a high price tag to your backsplash. They should be lit from behind with LED or comparable lighting to provide the maximum effect.

- **Resin:** Resin products also provide a translucent surface for backlit drama. They can be personalized with inserts like reeds, flowers, and other natural elements. Check the manufacturer's specifications (and local codes) for fire resistance, or plan a different material for the cooktop area.

above • Beadboard creates a classic country backsplash that's both affordable and easy to install, but should be supplemented with noncombustible elements behind the cooking surface.

above • Tile mosaics are both ancient and surprisingly modern. Now offered on mesh-mounted sheets, rather than as individual pieces, they're perfect for a wide range of kitchen styles and are easier for DIYers to install.

- **Mirror:** A mirrored backsplash can provide an easy-to-clean surface that reflects light and views.

- **Colored glass:** This can be backlit or just back-painted for drama. It's an easy-to-live-with material that will add a strong, contemporary focal point to your kitchen.

- **Beadboard:** Beadboard is an affordable, time-tested option for a country-inspired kitchen. Consider, though, whether cleaning splashed food out of its grooves is something you're prepared to take on and whether a noncombustible material should replace or cover it in the cooking-surface area for safety and local code compliance.

- **Brick or stone veneer:** Both can add rustic charm to your kitchen, especially in an oversize cooking-hearth area, but consider the challenging cleanup of rough surfaces and crevices.

- **Stainless steel:** This is a contemporary, easy-maintenance material for your backsplash, but may add more coolness and cost than your kitchen can afford.

top left • Resin materials can be enhanced with decorative inserts and lit from behind for a dramatic, customized backsplash.

left • Stainless steel offers a durable, low-maintenance surface for backsplashes, just as it does for countertops. It also reflects undercabinet lights for additional illumination.

DESIGN OPTIONS

You've determined whether your backsplash will be decorative, functional, or a combination of the two. You've considered the modern, traditional, or transitional style of your kitchen to inspire its composition. And you've decided on the material you want to use.

If it's the same material as your countertop, you have two design options: short or full height. When shorter versions are specified for a remodel to replace an existing 5-inch or 6-inch splash, it's helpful to go 1 inch above the current height to hide any drywall damage resulting from tearout.

If you're opting for tile, decorative paint, or resin with inserts, you have many more options and decisions to ponder. It's still crucial to factor in the other surfaces in the room. But you can be tremendously creative with blending shapes, colors, accents, and materials. Consider the practical as well as the pretty. Keep in mind the scale of focal-point elements vis-à-vis surrounding elements like range hoods.

When it comes to tile, standard field pieces will generally be far more affordable than accent pieces. You can create drama by alternating field-tile sizes and position—for instance, incorporating diagonally laid tiles in a rectangular frame—rather than relying solely on expensive accents to carry the design weight. Consider using some of the same material you chose for your floor tile in the backsplash for both continuity and savings. Large-format, coordinating rectangular tiles with widely spaced vertical pinstripe accents (or none at all) contribute to an updated look.

Backsplashes are ideal spots to show off your creative side and to splurge on a smaller scale.

right • Large-format tile is increasingly used in modern kitchen designs with dramatic effect. It offers the additional benefit of less grout maintenance, perfect for those messy areas behind cooktops.

Subway tile designs are widely used but can be combined with different colors, materials, and sizes for a more customized look.

above • Tile installed on the diagonal is a classic backsplash design that can be personalized with matching and coordinating accents.

above • Short splashes matching the countertop are among the most common and affordable.

left • Metallics add shimmer and style to a kitchen backsplash, especially when washed with lights from wall cabinets above.

STORAGE OPTIONS

There's no reason not to put the backsplash space to work, especially if your small kitchen lacks storage and counter space. Shallow wall shelves supported by brackets or niches are traditional options. Floating shelves offer more contemporary style. Both can hold mugs, spices, and oils and vinegars in attractive bottles.

Modular rail systems are becoming increasingly popular and widely available. They consist of a bar attached to the backsplash from which components can be hung. These components can provide a convenient spot for paper-towel holders, utensil bins, magnetized knife blocks, or small jars.

Another popular storage system is a tiled-in shelf or niche, especially in the cooktop area, for holding cooking supplies. Be sure that the heat-adjacent location won't damage the items you wish to store there.

Appliance garages are another backsplash storage option, especially for hiding small appliances like blenders or toasters when they're not in use.

Some cabinet lines offer built-in backsplash storage options. These can be shallow sliding-door spaces ideal for glasses and lit from within, or mini drawers designed for small elements like napkins, wine charms, corkscrews, and the like.

Pot racks are one way to add storage in and around the cooking zone. Though ceiling-mounted models are more common, wall-mounted versions also take advantage of untapped space.

top left · Flexible rail-based backsplash organizers let you customize storage to your needs and space, freeing up drawers and shelves while adding convenience to your meal preparation.

left · Groove-based organizers also take advantage of untapped backsplash potential, but offer a cleaner look for modern kitchens.

above · Tiled niches behind or next to a cooktop are traditional ways to add storage for small cooking-zone items.

A Personalized Backsplash

The owners of this custom home in Palo Alto, California, wanted the kitchen, like the rest of the house, to be very personal as well as pretty. After all, this would be the home in which they'd raise their children and build memories. The kitchen especially needed to be designed for the rigors of daily family living but look great while doing it.

The sun-drenched layout contributes to its charm and functionality. Drawer banks on every cabinet run, plus a pro-style gas range, vent hood, and refrigerator contribute convenience. The large windows and small-scale, wood-topped island warm up the space.

But the owners also wanted a kitchen that is uniquely theirs. This is clearly evident in the backsplash, which celebrates both their romantic love and cultural heritage. Each of their families' nations of origin are represented in the teacups selected, intermingled with their wedding china. The clever corners of the mosaic's tile frame are accented by teapot lids, and the front of a teapot is the centerpiece.

The same tile used throughout the kitchen is incorporated into the mosaic to tie the whole space together visually. The soft blue and china accents also provide a cheerful splash of color and whimsy to the traditional black, white, and wood kitchen. Every element in this custom backsplash was personally selected to please the homeowners' eyes and hearts and was expertly designed to enhance a classic kitchen.

above · **The personalized mosaic backsplash provides a sentimental focal point for this highly functional, classically designed family kitchen.**

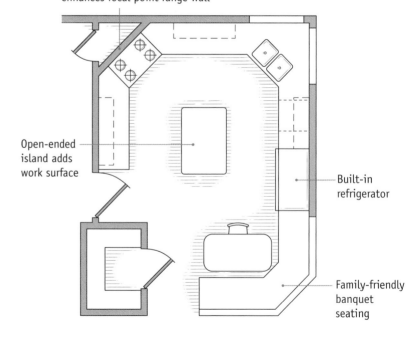

Custom mosaic backsplash enhances focal point range wall

Open-ended island adds work surface

Built-in refrigerator

Family-friendly banquet seating

top left • The neutral white, black, and wood tones let the blue backsplash take center stage in this traditional space.

above • A banquette next to the magnet-bedazzled refrigerator makes family meal time casual, convenient, and comfortable.

far left • The vintage-inspired pendants add a second whimsical note, as well as task lighting.

left • Decorative brackets enhance the charm of the painted white cabinetry.

FLOORING

Your kitchen floors should be as durable as they are stylish.

You may also want them to be comfortable underfoot and low maintenance.

Your choices have never been more plentiful than they are today.

Materials

Your kitchen floor will get harder use than probably any other flooring in your home. It will get splashed by your sink and nicked by utensils falling off of your range top. It'll have human, pet, and furniture feet dragged across it. It'll get skillets and schoolbooks dropped onto it. Your kitchen floor needs to be durable as well as attractive.

The good news is that there are a variety of materials available in just about every price range. Even traditionally expensive choices like wood and stone have decreased in price with import competition.

As with any material selection, it's important to make a choice based on how you'll use the space, not just how it looks. Consider whether your kitchen floor will get hard family use or lighter empty-nest activity. Do you cook for hours at a time, when softer flooring underfoot will be important? Do you love polished marble enough to maintain its shine and flawless beauty? All of these are important considerations in choosing the right floor for you.

If you're changing your kitchen floor while the other floors around it remain the same, you'll want to harmonize its look with the surrounding areas from which it's visible. You can mix tile in the kitchen with wood in the dining areas, for example, or wood in the kitchen with carpet in the adjacent family room, but they should coordinate or complement each other.

You can get this look from wood or high-quality laminates. Real woods can be refinished if damaged over time. Laminates can't, but they typically cost much less than wood.

You should also choose a floor that works with your home's value and neighborhood for resale purposes. If you're in an upscale area where most of the other houses feature stone tile, porcelain tile would be an acceptable substitute, but vinyl wouldn't meet local standards and could hurt your sale down the line.

Finally, when making your flooring purchase, it's best to order all that you'll need at one time, so that the finishes will be from the same production process. It's also best to factor in between 5 percent and 15 percent more material than your actual flooring size requires. Your installer or supplier can guide you as to the recommended allowance for your chosen material. This should leave you with some extra pieces for future repairs, if needed.

left • A wood floor can be solid or engineered. For kitchens sitting on concrete-slab foundations, engineered woods are typically the better installation choice.

above left and right • Tile is one of the most popular, durable kitchen flooring choices available today and can be natural stone, ceramic, or porcelain.

Planning Considerations

Replacing flooring in your kitchen entails some structural concerns, too.

The thickness of the new material is one key consideration. When you're replacing vinyl with tile or tile with solid wood, you're going to be introducing extra height into your space. Ensure that your refrigerator will still fit under the cabinet above, for instance, once the new flooring is installed. The extra ½ inch or more could easily erase the extra space you allowed between your counter-depth refrigerator's hinges and the wall cabinet above it.

Your new kitchen floor may also potentially lock your dishwasher into place so that it's unable to be serviced or replaced without damaging your new flooring. Talk to your flooring installer about running the material under at least the front legs and ensuring in advance that your machine's adjustable legs will accommodate the new height.

There are horizontal considerations, as well. A new wood or laminate floor calls for expansion gaps at the walls that your old baseboards might not cover. These issues must be addressed with a professional before you invest in new flooring. Many companies will provide and install new baseboards with your flooring. Be sure the style they offer fits your taste, and factor in the time and costs of having them painted, which some flooring companies won't do. If the new material—especially wood and laminate—is butting up to your existing cabinets, you will need molding to cover the necessary expansion gaps. You'll want to have this on hand for the flooring installation; again, factor in its installation cost. Be sure to ask the company selling you flooring if all of the necessary components and their installation are included, and ask them to point out each one on the quote.

You should also invest some time in researching the maintenance requirements to see if they fit your life-style. If, for example, you fell in love with polished marble in the showroom, consider the time involved in keeping it sealed and polished.

Like marble and travertine, wood floors—a popular choice today—require some ongoing TLC. You should wipe up spills as they occur to keep the floors from being damaged due to prolonged moisture exposure. If you're a busy parent and get to kitchen chores only after the young ones are in bed hours later, this might not be the best material for your kitchen. A distressed wood can work better for an active family seeking a more worry-free existence, where one more ding from your son's fire truck or your St. Bernard's claws will just add to its character, and the stain from last month's juice incident only enhances its warm tones.

above • Adding wood floors to an existing kitchen requires careful measuring and planning to avoid problems caused by the height difference of the new materials.

left • Tile installed wall to wall during a kitchen remodel, even under cabinets and appliances, will give the most finished look and fewest appliance replacement issues later.

When planning your flooring materials, consider their maintenance requirements. This Southwestern look can be created with easy-care porcelain or ceramic tile, rather than Saltillo, but a traditional dark gray grout would be more livable than white.

Matching New Flooring with Existing Spaces

In today's open-floor-plan homes, it's not uncommon to find the same wood or tile running through an entire level of your house. If you're changing all of the flooring—as is often the case in a whole-home remodel—your challenge will be to coordinate the new floor to cabinetry, countertops, and important furnishings in the entire space. You have similar challenges if you're changing just the kitchen flooring in an open-plan environment. When it will be seen from adjacent living and dining rooms, you're going to want the new flooring's colors and patterns to look good with what's in the entire space.

One designer tip to consider: Using one material throughout or minimizing visual contrasts between different flooring types will make the overall living space look larger. This could mean pairing your new maple or bamboo kitchen floors with a family room carpet in similar blonde tones.

When it comes to selecting new floors for an existing kitchen, pull visual cues from your countertops to select a color family that relates well. These are your two largest visual surfaces, so they should play well together. If your granite tops have strong tan flecks, a tan tile can work well. If your countertops have a busy pattern, go more neutral in your flooring. To complement your cabinets, floors should be one to two shades lighter or darker.

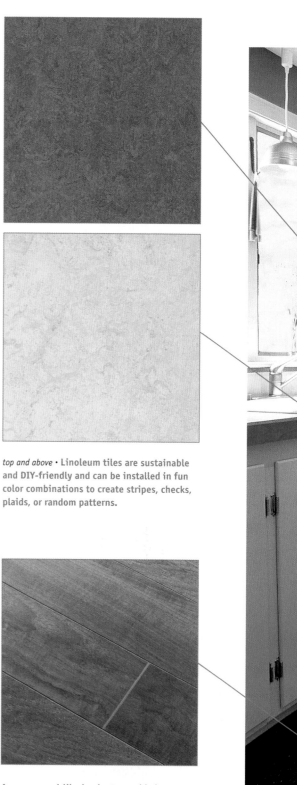

top and above • Linoleum tiles are sustainable and DIY-friendly and can be installed in fun color combinations to create stripes, checks, plaids, or random patterns.

A warm, wood-like laminate would also complement the countertop tones and can be installed by a skilled homeowner.

THE EXISTING ROOM

New flooring choices can easily improve the style and value of this affordable kitchen, currently covered in commercial vinyl tile.

Creamy porcelain tile will add durability, easy maintenance, and value to this kitchen, while making it seem more spacious by reducing visual contrast.

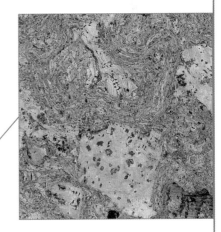

Natural cork will give years of comfortable use and complements the golden tones in the butcher block patterned countertops.

Wood and Wood Look-Alikes

Wood has long been a popular choice, especially in older houses. A solid wood floor that hasn't been affected by standing water could last for hundreds of years and add tremendous warmth and beauty to your home. It will likely extend from your kitchen throughout your main living areas, creating a unified expanse of natural beauty.

Traditionally, wood floors were finished in the home rather than at the lumberyard or mill. They were sanded, stained, and sealed by the flooring installer, requiring a skilled professional, lots of cleanup, and airing out of the house before the space could be enjoyed again. This is less true today because factories increasingly offer prefinished solid and engineered-wood floors. Both can be refinished in future years, with the solid models offering multiple refinishings and the engineered versions offering just one or two because of their thinner finished wood surface.

Solid hardwoods such as oak and maple are well suited to a kitchen's challenging environment. Solid softwoods like Douglas fir and pine will dent more easily, but many homeowners like the added distressing. It's possible to get a comparable distressed look now in an engineered floor as well.

Engineered-wood flooring has become an increasingly popular choice for several reasons. Perhaps most important, engineered-wood floors can be quickly and easily installed over the concrete slabs that form so many home foundations today because they are technically a "floating" floor. Solid wood's nail-down or glue-down installation isn't typically slab-friendly. In addition, engineered floors are generally less expensive to buy and install and are easy to maintain. Their installation is also DIY-friendly for a skilled homeowner.

top • Wood floors that are too distressed to be conventionally refinished can be painted for lasting charm.

above • Oak is a durable hardwood flooring choice for kitchens. Solid plank floors can be refinished numerous times, while engineered versions can be refinished far fewer, depending on their thickness.

left • Dramatic manufacturing improvements are making wood-look laminates and engineered-wood floors harder than ever to distinguish from solid wood floors.

below • Wood and wood-look floors are ideal for running from the kitchen into adjacent living areas, as they're comfortable to walk on and add both style and beauty to your home.

Bamboo floors are often sold in the same showrooms as engineered and solid wood floors, even though they come from fast-growing grasses, not trees. This makes them sustainable, though their adhesives and topcoats don't always make them eco-friendly. Early models dented and dinged easily, generating numerous homeowner complaints, but manufacturers have introduced more durable offerings, including strand bamboo, that are comparable to hardwoods.

Another wood-look alternative is laminate flooring. Like its engineered-wood competitors, laminate can be installed easily over concrete slabs and has an ultrahard factory finish. Its often-thinner structure can make it an easier replacement for tile in existing kitchens than wood. Set side by side, a high-quality laminate could easily pass for engineered wood, but it is actually just a picture of wood sandwiched between a substrate and topcoat. It can't be refinished even once. It can also be noisier to walk on than wood, but a good sound barrier can help minimize the noise.

below • Blonde wood floors can create a feeling of expansiveness in a kitchen and open living areas. They also show less pet hair, dust, and other hazards of daily living, offering a more family-friendly finish.

The wide-plank Douglas fir floor shows the beauty of this less-frequently selected wood species and was chosen to coordinate with the door and window frames.

above · Wood, laminate, and bamboo can all create this warm, golden floor suitable for traditional or modern kitchens.

left · Engineered-wood maple floors are stained dark for a rich, durable flooring choice.

Stone, Ceramic, and Porcelain Tiles

Tile floors are popular for their durability, beauty, and nearly endless design possibilities. Tile is a generic term that encompasses stone, ceramic, and porcelain materials produced in individual pieces rather than in sheets like vinyl. They come in varying sizes and shapes, most commonly square and rectangle, and in numerous increasingly large sizes. To use as flooring, the tile you select must be rated for floor use, with enough hardness and slip resistance to serve this purpose. The showroom sample and box will be marked accordingly.

STONE

Stone tiles are created from natural quarried materials, with granite, marble, limestone, travertine, and slate being especially popular for upscale floors. They are typically installed in large-format sizes with nearly imperceptible grout lines, contributing to the prized, seamless look of a natural stone floor. Many, however, are sensitive to acids and prone to etch or stain if spills are not cleaned immediately. Sealing helps but adds a regular maintenance chore. These factors, along with their high cost to purchase and install, have contributed to the increasing popularity of improved ceramic and porcelain tile offerings.

CERAMIC AND PORCELAIN

Like stone, ceramic and porcelain tiles are created from natural materials (clay, feldspar, and sand, in particular), but they are far more highly processed in order to become tile. New larger sizes, screen printing, and ink jet processes can make their surfaces nearly indistinguishable from natural stone.

Ceramic and porcelain tiles are like fraternal twins—typically made in the same factories using different varieties of the same materials and comparable manufacturing processes.

top • Large rectangles are becoming as popular as square for attractive, updated tile floor installations.

above • Tile floors create a hard, durable surface that can be tiring and painful to stand on for long stretches. Cushioned mats help alleviate some of the discomfort felt by back, feet, and legs.

right • Tile is one of the most versatile materials for creating unique flooring looks. Different colors, sizes, and shapes let you customize a kitchen to your desired style—from classic to kitsch.

The most significant differences are in consumer marketing; porcelain tile is often packaged with more designer features, like rectified edges and finishes that penetrate below the surface for better wear (see the sidebar on pp. 160–161), thus commanding a higher price. You can find similar offerings in ceramic tile, but they're less common.

Ceramic and porcelain tiles for residential use have been marred by wide grout lines. Not only is grout unattractive, but it also is a maintenance headache. It's best to use the largest tile size that works with the scale of your room and the darkest grout that closely matches it to help hide inevitable stains. You'll need to seal the grout before the new floor is used and periodically afterward. When possible, consider a tile with rectified edges, which are created by improved precision cutting processes and most commonly seen in more expensive porcelain offerings. These edges allow tiles to be installed so closely together that grout lines as tight as $\frac{1}{16}$ inch become nearly invisible.

There are a few drawbacks to a tile floor. First, any of these materials makes a floor that's hard underfoot. And some tiles—especially polished styles—can have a high slip factor. Antislip treatments that can be added to the floors after they are installed are available in most areas, but their professional application can add several dollars per square foot to your flooring. Finally, tile floors, especially those made from stone, are cool to the touch. Radiant heat, a coil system, that gets installed in the floor before the tiles go in, can offset this (see the sidebar on the facing page).

top • Terrazzo floors have come back in style, but the look today can also be achieved with rectified porcelain or ceramic tile.

right • This porcelain tile will give years of low-maintenance service and style to this hard-working kitchen.

Radiant Floor Heat

If you plan on replacing your kitchen floor, consider adding radiant floor heating at the same time. This system for heating a room from the bottom up is ideal for naturally cool floors like tile or stained concrete, but it's popular under wood and laminate in colder climates, too.

There are two types of radiant floor heating systems: electric, which uses cables, and hydronic, which uses water tubes. Both are embedded beneath the finished flooring to warm the room. Typically, electric is used if you're only going to install it in one room, but it is a more energy-intensive system. You can reduce costs by programming your radiant heat system to operate only when you need it—for the time you spend in your kitchen before you head to work, for example—on a thermostat independent of your home's forced-air system.

Recent innovations have combined all of the radiant system components that go below your finished floor into easy-to-install panels, cutting the time and cost involved with having one. There are even models suitable for installing below a floating engineered wood or laminate floor or for embedding in thinset cement overlays for a new concrete floor.

If you're building a new home or undergoing a whole-house remodel, hydronic radiant heat can be among the most energy efficient, comfortable, and healthy heating systems available today.

This look can come from costly natural stone or from porcelain or ceramic tiles for a more affordable, lower-maintenance surface.

The New Porcelain Tiles

Porcelain isn't a particularly new tile material. How it's being designed, manufactured, and marketed today, however, is bringing tremendous new innovation and style to the category.

• **Smooth edges for tiny grout lines:** New manufacturing techniques allow porcelain tile to be installed with grout lines as tight as $\frac{1}{16}$ inch. In addition to offering an easier-to-maintain flooring surface, these rectified edges offer a more versatile, upscale, natural-looking floor.

• **Color penetration for greater wear resistance:** New manufacturing technologies that can push surface color and pattern deep into semiglazed tile means that chips and dents barely show. The minor damage that can typically result from kitchen mishaps will show far less until you have an opportunity to replace the damaged tile.

• **Fabric, stone, and wood look-alikes:** Another style advance is the ability to produce porcelain tile that looks like fabric, natural stone, or wood, bringing new design options to the kitchen that are otherwise impractical. These new tiles create versatile high-end looks that are also worry-free, low maintenance, and super-durable, perfect for a busy family kitchen.

• **Ultrathin tiles for faster, cleaner installation:** Some porcelain manufacturers are now producing ultrathin tiles. These exceptionally skinny but strong tiles can be installed directly over existing flooring, reducing mess and the landfill while saving time and cleanup. They require an extra installation step, so your tile installer needs to know that you requested ultrathin tiles when bidding your job.

Today's new porcelain tiles can create a wood-look floor that doesn't mind water.

Dramatic patterns and shapes are all achievable in new porcelain tile offerings.

above • Grout lines and grout maintenance are minimized for a cool, clean look in rectified tile.

right • The texture, as well as the color and pattern, of distressed wood can now be captured in durable porcelain.

Alternative Materials

There are myriad other possibilities for your kitchen flooring beyond wood and tile.

CONCRETE

Stained concrete is an extremely versatile floor that can be polished for a contemporary look or faux-finished for a traditional one. You can also personalize it with custom "rugs" or borders to highlight a table or island, or add just about any color or pattern that ties into your decor. Concrete is an ideal floor for indoor–outdoor living; you can extend it onto a patio for a unified design and a floor that handles wet and sandy feet with ease. It is hard underfoot and will need to be kept sealed if you want to maintain a perfect finish.

CORK, LINOLEUM, AND RUBBER

Cork, linoleum, and rubber are all soft underfoot and ideal for busy home cooks who want a comfortable workspace. Cork and linoleum are also ideal for those with allergy issues and sustainability concerns.

- **Cork** is made from the bark of the cork tree and is harvested without sacrificing the tree. In addition to being antimicrobial, it is also insulating—adding to your home's energy efficiency—and fire- and insect-resistant. Although cork floors are quiet underfoot and excellent from a comfort standpoint, there are a few maintenance issues that may be challenging for a senior or busy homeowner. Cork needs to be sealed when installed, then every few years afterward; it requires special cleaning products for heavy cleaning, which should be applied as soon as a spill occurs, and requires regular damp mopping. Water and other liquids can damage cork over time.

above • Cork offers numerous earth- and family-friendly benefits, but it does require ongoing maintenance to maintain its natural beauty.

below • Sustainable, comfortable, and healthy, linoleum is a versatile flooring material ideal for kitchens and living areas.

• **Linoleum** is another flooring option worth considering. Like cork, it's sustainable, hypoallergenic, quiet, and comfortable to stand on. Many of our grandparents' kitchens were covered in this family-friendly material that got passed by in the flooring trends of the last few decades. It's enjoying a resurgence with active, eco-friendly households thanks to its green credentials and old-fashioned charm. Linoleum can be installed in sheets, which often gets it confused with less-durable vinyl, or in tiles that can be replaced if damaged. Upscale linoleum installations often combine colors in contemporary or retro-chic patterns.

• **Rubber** is also eco-friendly and soft underfoot. Like linoleum, it can be installed in DIY-friendly, replaceable tiles and comes in many patterns and colors. Its drawbacks deserve serious consideration, though: Some rubbers are flammable or react poorly to oil, which is commonly used in cooking. Rubber may also cause allergic reactions.

top • A seamless indoor–outdoor flooring look like this can be achieved with versatile concrete.

left • Rubber is a low-maintenance, ultra comfortable kitchen floor to stand and work on for long periods.

Flooring

WOOD AND BAMBOO
$$ to $$$

- Solid wood floors offer long life and almost endless refinishing possibilities, but can't be installed in all kitchens.

- Solid wood floors are generally the thickest material you can install in your kitchen, entailing especially careful measuring for appliance and cabinet fit.

- Wood floors are available in sustainable species harvested from protected forests. The ability to refinish them adds both longevity and sustainability. Clear topcoats for finished-on-site floors add gloss, if desired, and a protective layer. Older floors are sometimes painted in nontraditional colors or patterns rather than refinished for extended life and a creative touch.

- Many wood floors on the market today are prefinished, engineered products, with a protective layer on top, finished wood just below, and an unfinished substrate.

- Engineered wood can be floated over concrete slab floors in most homes, making it a versatile choice.

- Oak, cherry, maple, beech, walnut, and birch are popular in both solid and engineered-wood floors.

- Wide plank styles are very popular, with 5 inches being the most common in this category. Wider styles from 8 inches to 12 inches are available at premium pricing, more typically in engineered than solid wood.

- Durable bamboo floors often look like their wood counterparts but are made from fast-growing grasses, not trees.

- Bamboo has traditionally been more ding and dent prone than wood, but new finishing techniques and strand bamboo offerings have overcome that shortcoming.

- Wood and bamboo are both comfortable to stand on.

LAMINATE
$ to $$

- Laminate floors may look like wood (or any other material they're imitating, like stone), but they're actually a repeated image of that surface under a protective finish.

- Laminate floors can typically be installed where engineered wood floors can go and are generally less expensive.

- Laminate floors offer excellent durability because of their protective finish, but they can't be refinished if damaged.

- Laminate floors generally offer very easy maintenance.

- Most laminate floors employ a click-lock installation system that's DIY friendly.

- Their warranties compare to engineered woods, typically 15 years or longer.

Solid and engineered woods are a natural for open-floor-plan kitchens, as they transition smoothly between work and play spaces.

CERAMIC AND PORCELAIN TILE
$ to $$$

- Ceramic tile is one of the most widely available and affordable flooring materials.

- Properly installed, glazed ceramic and porcelain tile are impervious to surface stains and moisture.

- Both are offered in a broad range of shapes, styles, and sizes that can be used together to create unique floors with borders, inlays, and other customized looks.

- Color body finishes, most commonly seen in higher-price-point porcelains, penetrate the surface image deep into the tile, providing greater protection against visual damage.

- Rectified formats, also most commonly offered on higher-priced porcelains, allow for much narrower grout lines between tiles.

- Both are extremely hard underfoot and can cause foot, leg, hip, and back stress when working on them for extended periods.

- Their hardness will often cause breakage to glasses or dishes that drop onto ceramic or porcelain tile floors.

- Neither glazed porcelain nor ceramic tile needs to be sealed, but you may want to seal the grout between the tiles periodically for greater stain protection. The frequency will depend on how much traffic your kitchen gets.

Ceramic and porcelain tile can evoke wood, brick, or natural stone with impressive realism.

DIY-friendly vinyl tiles can mimic a stone or ceramic tile floor at a very affordable price.

NATURAL STONE
$$$

- One of the most ancient and beautiful flooring materials in the world, popular natural stone floors include granite, slate, marble, and travertine.
- Should be professionally installed for optimum results.
- Part of natural stone's beauty derives from its naturally occurring variations; color and pattern fluctuations from tile to tile are a feature, not a flaw.
- Large-format tiles (typically 18 inches or 24 inches square and 12 inches by 24 inches or 36 inches rectangular) and mosaic sheets are both popular.
- Natural stone should be regularly sealed for better stain protection. The frequency of sealing will depend on the stone selected and the traffic level of your kitchen. Your showroom adviser or contractor will provide the optimum schedule for your selection and environment.
- Polished natural stone will need to be periodically polished, as well.
- Like ceramic and porcelain tile, natural stone is extremely cold and hard underfoot.

CORK
$$ to $$$

- Natural and sustainable.
- Available in numerous finishes and styles, from casual squares to classic herringbone.
- Naturally insect repellant, sound and temperature insulating, and fire resistant; ideal for those with mold, dust mite, and other household allergies.
- Soft to stand on for extended periods of time.
- Requires gentle, regular cleaning with special cleaning products, as dirt, dust, debris, and harsh household cleaners can damage its surface.
- Needs to be sealed when installed and again every few years.

VINYL AND LINOLEUM
$ to $$

- Widely available and easy to install in tile format.
- Vinyl tile and sheets are both affordable floor options for budget remodels.
- Low-cost vinyl is prone to corner curling and fading in the sun.
- Sheet vinyl and linoleum should be professionally installed for best results.
- Both are soft to stand on for extended periods.
- Linoleum, often confused with less-expensive vinyl, is a durable, sustainable flooring material made from linseed oil and other natural ingredients.

CONCRETE
$$

- Often takes advantage of the kitchen's existing slab surface.
- Offers tremendous variety in colors, patterns, finishes, and styles for both traditional and contemporary kitchens.
- Typically sealed against staining, except when a distressed, historical look is desired.
- Ideal surface for extending into outdoor patios adjacent to the kitchen, especially in waterfront situations.
- Impervious to moisture.
- Hard and cold to stand on for extended periods and likely to crack dishes or glasses that fall on it.
- Can be warmed up with radiant floor heat, if desired.
- Can be customized with artwork, symbols, text, or concrete rugs to personalize a space.

New Floor Meets Old in Open-Plan Kitchen

Shortly after the homeowners bought this 1980s northern California ranch, they replaced all of the home's flooring. Years later, they wanted to update the kitchen into a more open floor plan that connected it to a dining nook and family room, but they didn't want to replace all of their flooring again.

With the help of a creative kitchen designer, they ended up with a great-looking, hard-working new kitchen that opens wide to the rest of their home while preserving as much of the flooring as possible.

The tile that had been chosen years before was no longer available. So while some of the existing tile stayed in the kitchen for continuity and cost savings, the design team created a tile mosaic border and then set new coordinating field tile within the new border on a diagonal. This assisted the design in several ways. First, the grout changes between old and new floors were de-emphasized by the border. Second, the new tile installed on the diagonal created a design focal point, and the different sizes between old and new tiles reinforced that point.

The homeowners had 10 extra replacement tiles from their first flooring redo, and they came in handy. When original tiles were removed to create the new kitchen floor, some of them damaged adjacent tiles in the process. The replacements came to the rescue at that point.

To unify the new tile with the kitchen even more, the designer repeated the mosaic border tile in the backsplash.

The end result is an updated new kitchen—and kitchen floor—that blends beautifully with the existing home.

This traditional kitchen remodel that improved the home's traffic flow and style was achieved with minimal disruption to the existing tile floor. New coordinating tiles were added only where necessary to complete the project.

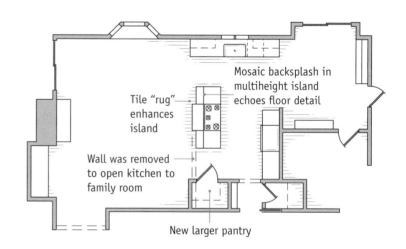

Mosaic backsplash in multiheight island echoes floor detail

Tile "rug" enhances island

Wall was removed to open kitchen to family room

New larger pantry

The new tiles create a flooring focal
point to embrace the new kitchen island.

above • The backsplash's mosaics and creamy field tile get
their inspiration from the new and old floor materials.

above • New tile meets old with historic flair and
professional attention to detail.

above • The areas where new tile was needed got a mosaic
border to unite the two areas with creative detail.

SINKS AND

Your kitchen sink and faucet get more use than any others in your home.

They wash pots and pans, produce, hands, babies, and the occasional small pet.

Choose models that work for how you'll really use them.

FAUCETS

The Critical Kitchen Sink

The kitchen sink is so essential to our daily lives that it's even become a cliché: *They threw in everything but the kitchen sink.* But you know that there's nothing cliché about choosing a sink when creating a new kitchen for your home.

If you're not limited by existing cabinetry or countertops, your choices are vast. Start by considering how many bowls you need and their relative size. This should be determined by the tasks you perform at the sink and the amount of counter space you're willing to dedicate to it. Every inch you give your sink is an inch less of usable countertop.

If you want a garbage disposal at the sink, you might want to dedicate a small sink bowl to it, or install the disposal in a second prep sink where you'll chop vegetables and create other disposal-friendly waste. If you regularly hand-wash large items in your kitchen sink, a single or large-small bowl combination (often called one and three-quarters) could be ideal.

Once you've determined the configuration that makes sense for how you'll use your sink or sinks, consider the material you want. Style, as well as functionality, plays a role here. Some sinks, like stainless steel and composites, offer low maintenance but have a contemporary look. Others, like fireclay and copper, look more traditional. Weigh all attributes carefully if you're considering an integral, farmhouse, or undermount sink. These are much more challenging to change later than a drop-in model.

top right · **This undermount sink is purposely understated to allow the countertop cabinetry and hardware, and leaded-glass doors to take center stage.**

bottom right · **Granite composites bring low-maintenance durability to the kitchen sink.**

The white apron front sink is a classic for traditional and transitional kitchens.

Sink Types and Materials

TOP-MOUNT/DROP-IN/SELF-RIMMING
$

- Widely available in hardware and home-center stores.
- Typically easy or even do-it-yourself installation.
- Most commonly used with laminate countertops.
- Precut holes on the sink ledge for faucet installation.
- Top-mount edge makes cleanup time-consuming, though newer micro-edge styles minimize the bulk and extra effort.
- Broad selection of materials, styles, and sizes, but most common is 33-inch double bowl for standard sink base cabinet.
- Top-mount stainless sink models, usually purchased for budget remodels, are often less-expensive, thinner models that are noisier and harder to clean than their undermount counterparts.
- Acrylic sinks' glossy finishes can be easily damaged but are repairable.
- Traditional enamel over cast iron and steel are also widely available in top-mount sinks; the enamel over steel is lighter and more affordable but noisier and more chip-prone.
- Some composite undermounts have a finished rim and faucet drilling that allow them to be installed as top mounts. They are sometimes identified as dual-mount.

UNDERMOUNT
$$ to $$$

- Widely available in home-center and plumbing specialty stores.
- Broadest selection of all sink types in terms of materials, styles, configurations, and sizes.
- Faucets typically mount on countertop with undermount sink installation.
- Designer styling and easier cleanup than drop-in styles.
- Require professional installation and difficult to replace later.
- Higher-quality, quieter, 16-gauge and 18-gauge stainless-steel models are available for undermounting.
- Low-maintenance composites, made from a blend of granite or quartz particles for durability, are increasingly available.
- Many specialty sinks—like triple bowl, modular styles with drain boards and accessories included, or exotic materials like copper—are made for undermount installation.

above • Undermount sinks are commonly installed in natural and engineered-stone countertops.

INTEGRAL
$$ to $$$

- Most often paired with Corian or comparable solid-surface countertops.
- Solid-surface integral sinks are stain resistant and can be sanded by homeowner for nick or scratch repair.
- Same material as solid-surface tops but not always available in same colors—often white or other popular neutrals only.
- Imperceptible seam between sink and countertop offers sleek style and easier maintenance.
- Typically allow for integral drain board.
- Also used with concrete and soapstone countertops in same colors and patterns.
- Increasing availability of integral sinks in engineered-stone and porcelain slab counters.

FARMHOUSE/APRON STYLE
$$$

- Most often found in plumbing specialty stores.
- Typically selected when entire kitchen is being remodeled; impractical to retrofit into a standard sink base cabinet.
- Most often used in traditional and transitional settings.
- Somewhat limited selection of materials, styles, and configurations.
- Most common are durable fireclay and enamel models, but stainless steel is finding its way into transitional kitchens.
- Specialty materials like copper, bronze, and soapstone are specified for higher-end kitchens but come with maintenance requirements to maintain their natural beauty.
- Exposed face sometimes damaged by objects rubbing or banging against it.

This apron-front sink blends seamlessly with the countertop.

Updating Fixtures in Existing Kitchens

Faucets break, parts become unavailable, and sinks chip or crack. You may find yourself needing to replace one or both without wanting to take on a full remodel. This is an excellent opportunity to add style and functionality to your kitchen.

If you have laminate countertops and a top-mounted sink, replacing the sink is fairly simple. So is replacing a faucet for such a sink, as long as the new model doesn't require more holes than the existing sink offers. If the new faucet requires fewer holes, the extra ones can be covered with a soap dispenser and/or hole cap by your local plumber. Replacing a faucet can give you the opportunity to add pullout, multiple-stream, sensor, or other features that your old model didn't include. You can also replace an older faucet with one that better reflects current styles, ideally in keeping with your overall kitchen aesthetic.

Many top-mount sinks available at home centers are made for a standard 33-inch cutout and just require skilled installation. There are new undermounting sinks and systems for laminate countertops; be sure your installer is skilled and experienced in this application to avoid the many potential problems possible with a faulty installation.

The most common sink and faucet replacements occur when you're replacing your countertops. If your chosen tops are Corian, you can opt for a standard top-mount model, undermount installation, or an integral sink. Many homeowners like the sleek style and easy cleanup of integral sinks made of the same material as the countertop. Some take advantage of the countertop replacement to add an integral, sloped drain board as well. These can also be incorporated into concrete and certain stainless-steel tops.

If your chosen tops are natural stone, porcelain slab, or engineered stone (marketed as Caesarstone, Sile-stone, and others), you're likeliest to choose an undermount sink, although there is an increasing availability of sinks in the same material that can be installed as integral. Your only limitation in this instance is the size of the existing base cabinet. You can opt for a double or single bowl, whichever is best suited to your needs.

You can replace a faucet for an undermount or integral faucet as easily as a top-mount model, but hole count matters more, as caps are designed for the deck plate that comes with top-mount installations rather than for sitting directly on a countertop. If you choose a three-hole faucet for a countertop drilled for four, a soap dispenser can fill the last hole and add functionality to your cleanup zone.

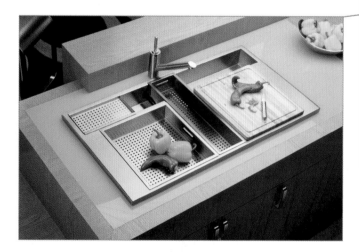

This sleek top-mount stainless steel sink is loaded with prep and clean-up accessories.

THE EXISTING ROOM

This budget remodel can get a style and functionality boost from a new sink and faucet. Both are easy upgrades in the existing laminate countertops.

A faucet with hands-free operation and a pull-out spray head adds tremendous functionality to the sink area.

It is now possible to undermount certain sinks in laminate tops for easier cleanup and enhanced style.

A granite composite sink will not chip or scratch the way the original sink can, and it also can be undermounted if the homeowners decide to use it with an upgraded countertop later.

The Second Sink

Many larger kitchens today—especially those with islands—have a second sink. There are numerous benefits to this amenity, including allowing two adults to cook together more easily, convenience to the stovetop, and creating the ability to better zone your kitchen for food preparation, cleanup, food storage, and cooking tasks.

If you decide on a second sink, the best location for it is in the prep zone. It is likely to be a smaller version of your main kitchen sink, intended for washing fruits and vegetables rather than for cleanup. Ideally, it's located in a spot that's an arm's reach from the cooking surface. This means fewer steps with boiling pots of water or cutting boards loaded down with heaping stew ingredients.

Your second sink can have a disposal for safe food waste, if desired. It can also have a full-size pullout faucet or, more likely, a smaller bar-size faucet that matches your main sink's model in style and finish.

Though generally a step saver for large spaces, even an average-size kitchen can benefit from a second sink if it's regularly used by two cooks simultaneously.

top · Second sinks are often used for entertaining at home, as this ice bucket stand-in amply demonstrates.

right · Locating a prep sink in or near the cooking zone creates a more efficient work flow in a large kitchen.

above • A second sink is often selected from the same material as the main version, even exotics like copper.

left • A second sink may serve the bar area rather than the kitchen itself.

Two Sinks for a Two-Cook Kitchen

This contemporary British Columbia kitchen looks right at home in the custom, Pacific-inspired home built around it. The owners are gourmet chefs who love to cook together, so having a space that was both highly functional and fabulously stylish was crucial to them.

The homeowners wanted a visual flow that tied the kitchen to the home and landscape to inspire them when they prepare the local ingredients they love to cook. Submerged lake birch was used throughout the kitchen. The sculptural breakfast bar shares the great room's concrete fireplace style and material. And the infinity island—topped in stunning, as well as sensible, glass—was inspired by the infinity lap pool outside.

Two sinks are important to this chef couple. The stainless-steel prep sink at the end of the island is convenient to both the cooktop and the ovens on the perimeter, creating an uninterrupted workspace for the person cooking. Within easy reach of the refrigerator is the main sink with its restaurant-style faucet. One sink overlooks the beautiful outdoor view, whereas the other allows for conversation with guests.

All in all, this scenery-inspired kitchen works for nourishing the cooks' spirit while they nourish guests with the meals they turn out.

A tall restaurant-style faucet and deep stainless sink handle large pots with ease.

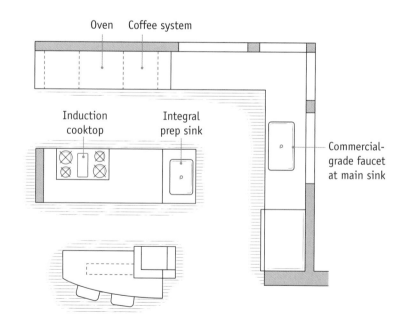

Oven   Coffee system

Induction cooktop

Integral prep sink

Commercial-grade faucet at main sink

above · A new-age induction cooktop sits in a countertop crafted from an old world material— textured glass.

top left · The shapes and finishes in this airy, gourmet kitchen were inspired by the home's natural surroundings.

left · An integral stainless-steel prep sink near the cooktop is the perfect spot for emptying boiling water with a minimum of steps.

Faucet Basics

Faucets are almost as varied as the kitchens in which they live and should be attractive as well as functional. There is a fantastic selection of traditional, transitional, and contemporary styles and configurations; prices range from less than $100 at a discount store up to $1,000 for a specialty fixture. The more expensive models tend to offer more features and better durability. You can find single-handle, double-handle, pullout spray, or side-spray choices in most price categories. These are largely personal preferences based on the look and convenience you desire.

FEATURES

Before making a decision about a faucet, first determine which features are important to your regular kitchen routines:

- A pull-out sprayer with multiple flow settings?

- A matching soap dispenser?

- A high-arcing restaurant style for cleaning large pots?

- Hands-free or tap on/off operation to reduce germ spread and cross-contamination of food?

- Built-in filtration?

MOUNTING

One factor in your faucet decision that is often over-looked is mounting. A faucet installed on a stone or solid-surface countertop should be able to mount directly to the top; the optional deck plate that comes with it is designed for sitting on top-mount sinks. If your plumbing hook-ups are wall-mounted, you'll want to find a compatible faucet, unless you have a local professional who can drill into your installed counters (difficult on stone and risky on tile).

above · A tall copper faucet works well for washing pots in the deep sink, while its matching companion dispenses hot water on demand.

left · The pull-out spray head on this faucet adds convenience to cleaning the sink and its contents.

right · A bridge faucet imparts traditional style to an old world-inspired kitchen.

MATERIALS

The decorative finish on your faucet may be oil-rubbed bronze, stainless steel, composite black, polished chrome, or a variety of other looks. The glossier it is, the more you'll be wiping water spots and fingerprints from its surface. A PVD (physical vapor deposition) finish, which bonds the color to the faucet, will better protect your faucet from corrosion and discoloration.

The faucet's interior mechanisms will probably be made from solid brass, a brass blend, or stainless steel. Solid brass and stainless hold up better than blends to high pressure and hot water. They will also cost more. The faucet's moving parts that control water temperature and flow are likely to be ceramic disks. The better quality they are, the smoother they glide and the more control you have over volume and temperature. Ceramic disks are also more durable and less leak prone than inexpensive faucet o-rings.

above • Stainless steel is a popular, durable, low-maintenance kitchen faucet finish.

below • A brass finish is often selected to deliver traditional elegance to a classic kitchen.

Checklist for a Perfect Faucet Fit

- For an undermount sink, position the faucet holes so that they clear the hidden sink-rim edge.

- For a top-mount sink, match the faucet and the accessories to the number of holes drilled in the sink rim. Check the hole spacing carefully if you want a two-handle faucet. If you need to cover extra holes, choose a faucet that offers a base plate or add accessories like a soap dispenser or hole cover.

- Consider clearances behind the sink. Do the faucet controls need room at the back for the arc of the control lever or for lever handles? Does the spout location pose any problem? You can offset a single-control faucet to a corner of the sink to eliminate interference with window hardware or a raised bar.

- Extra-thick counters, such as those made of stone, wood, or concrete, can present a problem for deck-mounted faucets if the mounting system doesn't have enough reach. Make sure that the shank length accommodates the counter thickness or that there is a compatible extender available for your installation.

- Make sure you've got reach. Does the faucet spout swivel in a wide enough arc to reach all the sink bowls? Two-handle faucets, including bridge-style faucets, might not work with some double-bowl sinks.

top left · Brushed nickel is a popular finish that complements a variety of kitchen styles.

left · Oil-rubbed bronze is another old-world finish that has gained popularity in traditional as well as transitional kitchens.

Hands-Free Faucets

Sensor faucets have come a long way from those we find in public restrooms. There's a new breed with the same water-saving benefits, but improved style and functionality, for your kitchen.

Because your kitchen faucet can be ground zero for spreading germs as well as food contaminants, turning one on and off without hands can be a healthy alternative.

The new hands-free faucets are available in motion-sensor operation, where you put your hands below the spout and water starts flowing at whatever temperature setting you chose for its last use, or with tap on/off technology. This latter method means touching the faucet anywhere on its body with an elbow or arm to start the water flow. This works wonderfully when your hands are coated in chicken or you're carrying a hot pot and don't have a free hand.

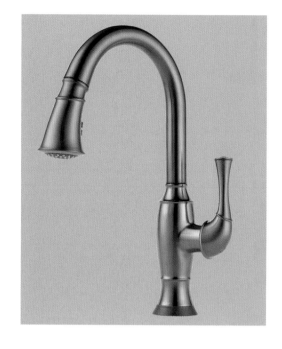

right and below • The convenience and popularity of hands-free faucet operation has led to a wider selection in configurations and finishes.

top left · Hands-free operation and a stainless finish help faucets stay cleaner.

above right · A tap of your arm starts and stops the faucet, an ideal convenience when your hands are busy or covered in food.

left · The hands-free operation on this polished chrome finish means fewer fingerprints to wipe off.

POT FILLERS

Pot fillers are specialized faucets mounted near your cooking surface to assist in filling large, heavy pots at their point of use. They're typically added during a full-scale remodel. Although they save you the heavily laden trip from the sink to the burner, unless you have a sink installed nearby you'll be making the return trip to the sink if your food requires draining.

If you find a pot filler convenient, choose one in a finish that matches your other kitchen faucets. They look best between a range hood and countertop rather than in the shorter space afforded by an over-the-range microwave. Newer pot fillers that mount in an island or peninsula countertop are also available.

GARBAGE DISPOSALS

Garbage disposals can be convenient for getting rid of certain food waste. When kept clean themselves, they'll reduce the unpleasant smell of your kitchen garbage can between trips to the curb. Disposals have been created that can work with your home's septic system if you're not on city sewers.

Most disposals, septic and standard, work on a continuous-feed basis. You turn them on and off with a switch installed in the countertop or cabinet or on the wall. There are batch-feed disposals that work when you insert a special stopper into the disposal opening and turn it. Both systems have the same effectiveness, but some professionals feel that the batch-feed system reduces the chance of injury or the chance of non-food items falling in.

top • Wall-mounted pot fillers are the most common style of this cooking zone appliance.

right • Pot fillers keep you from carrying a heavy pot to your cooking surface, but a drain is still required to empty the water somewhere else in the kitchen.

Water Filtration and Hot-Water Dispensers

If you love purified water or hot water on demand, you may opt for a water-filtration system or hot-water dispenser at your kitchen sink. Water-filtration systems may be integrated into your main kitchen faucet or dispensed through their own spigot. Finding styles that work with more upscale traditional and transitional kitchens has been challenging; higher-end faucets with that feature built in are a more appealing option for these homes.

On-demand hot water for tea or soup is desirable to many homeowners. Both hot-water and water-filtration dispensers typically involve installing equipment in the cabinet below the sink. If your space is very limited, it's best to consult with a professional before investing in either purchase or installation.

above · An instant hot-water dispenser is a tremendous convenience for instant coffee, soup, and tea lovers.

top left · If your cooktop is located on an island or peninsula, a deck-mounted pot filler can be a helpful addition to your kitchen.

left · A second, matching faucet for your water-filtration system brings an added convenience and health benefit to your kitchen.

DECORATIVE

Decorative touches often provide more than decoration to your kitchen. The lights, window coverings, and seating you choose impact both functionality and comfort. And the paint color and personal elements you select delight your senses.

TOUCHES

Finishing Your Kitchen

Decorative touches are often selected at the end of a kitchen remodel even though planning for some of these last-to-be-added elements, including lighting and display cabinetry, should be built into your design process. Decorative elements can entail customization, like sewing banquette cushions and making window coverings, so their costs, time frame, and trades should not be overlooked in the budgeting process. Other elements included in this catch-all category include wall coverings, throw rugs, baskets and bins, and decorative dishware and artwork.

A kitchen that includes well-thought-out decorative touches not only creates a place where you want to spend time but one that is also functional and comfortable for family and friends also.

above • Lighting, paint, furniture, and accessories complete and personalize your kitchen.

left • Window coverings should provide privacy and glare reduction, as well as adding coordinating style to your space.

left · Choose your furnishings and fabrics with an eye to durability, as well as style, in the demanding kitchen environment.

A Farmhouse Kitchen without Cliché

Sometimes a kitchen remodel is just a one-room update. Other times the new kitchen is part of a whole-house remodeling project, as was the case with this 1920s Oakland, California, residence. The new owners, a sculptor and Latin teacher, loved its location, but there was no love lost for the home's dated floor plan or dark, closed-in kitchen.

The list of must-haves included converting a bedroom into a breakfast room/artist studio, adding a deck, updating the dining room, and renovating the kitchen with a more open floor plan. Befitting the large property's chicken coop and vegetable garden and the couple's love of local crafts and urban farming, a farm-style kitchen was designed, but with a personalized, modern flair.

The new space functions well as a sunny farmhouse kitchen, especially as its second sink is a utility basin standing immediately off of the garden entrance, but it also flows seamlessly into the rest of the home.

Flanking the range are open shelves, because the home chef wanted the easiest access possible to her cooking supplies. But softening their modern appeal are the sculpted brackets below as well as beadboard detail. In another nod to the traditional, butcher block countertops were installed in the cooking prep zone, and they stylishly complement the more contemporary concrete countertops surrounding the sink.

As in classic farmhouse kitchens across the country, a table and wooden chairs sit nearby for catching up with friends, art projects, or local news, but the dual-pane Douglas fir windows letting Western sunlight stream in are contemporary California. The kitchen's new primary sink and traditional bridge faucet look onto a new dining room pass-through, which also lets the sun warm all areas in the space.

Although the updated kitchen still feels intimate and cozy, it tripled in size with the adjacent artist studio/breakfast room conversion. But best of all, perhaps, is that the walls are lovingly adorned with the homeowners' artwork and flowers grown in their gardens.

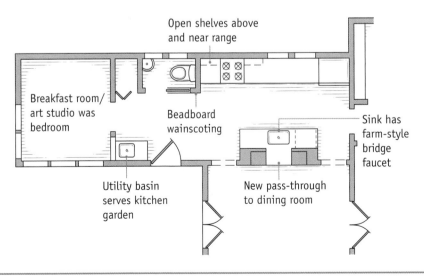

top left · **This personalized kitchen blends wood and concrete, paint and stain, country and contemporary, flair and functionality in a savvy remodel.**

bottom left · **A unique basin serves as the kitchen's second sink and makes a handy spot for washing produce picked from the vegetable garden.**

above · **The homeowner wanted the convenience of open shelving in her cooking zone. Decorative brackets and beadboard backing dress it up.**

top right · **A new pass-through between the kitchen and dining area adds light to both spaces and enhances social gatherings.**

Open shelves above and near range

Breakfast room/ art studio was bedroom

Beadboard wainscoting

Sink has farm-style bridge faucet

Utility basin serves kitchen garden

New pass-through to dining room

Designing a Well-Lit Kitchen

Too often, lighting is considered an afterthought and is underbudgeted. Don't make this mistake in your kitchen design planning. First and foremost, lighting needs to be functional; it also can add a decorative element to your kitchen. When designed well, you'll hardly notice it beyond attractive fixtures. Done poorly, you'll do a disservice to your investment and the kitchen's workability.

When planning your kitchen, consider where you'll be cleaning dishes, using knives, measuring flour, and reading cookbooks, and add task lighting above those spots. If they face out into the room, you'll probably opt for decorative fixtures at those locations. Be sure they're properly scaled and sited to your workspace. Some mini-pendants are intended more as accents than task lighting, for instance.

If you're placing a downdraft hood behind an island or peninsula cooktop, select a light fixture overhead that will give you enough light but won't be impacted by cooking gases or steam not captured by the downdraft.

Take advantage of natural light with window coverings that allow the light to bathe your kitchen with warmth and sunshine. (You might also want to consider a professionally applied film to protect your space and its contents from damaging UV rays.) If your kitchen doesn't have enough windows and adding more isn't practical, a skylight can be a great addition for single-story homes. Tubular models are an ideal option, as they are the sleekest (looking like large recessed lights in your ceiling) and the most cost-effective to install. They are even DIY friendly.

Be sure you have enough general room light for enjoying your kitchen at night. Recessed lighting is commonplace, but some ceilings, especially older vaulted versions, don't allow for this. Other options for general lighting include track lighting, monorails, and cable lighting.

Interior cabinet lights make their contents glow and add tremendously to the luxurious appeal of built-ins.

Task lighting at seating locations like tables and islands should be both decorative and functional.

above • The vent hood insert provides crucial task lighting for the cooking surface.

Track lighting can be installed on beams or directly to a ceiling. Unlike older models, new offerings include sleek, compact track heads in popular shapes and finishes designed to coordinate with your kitchen's other elements.

Cable systems are similar to tracks in that they position individual light fixtures where they're needed, but these fixtures run on thin, suspended cables rather than flat tracks. This lighting style works best in a contemporary space, like a loft.

Monorail lighting systems are also similar to track lighting, but they are bendable into curves, giving you more design flexibility, and may be suspended from the ceiling or run flat against it. With monorails and tracks, it's not uncommon to have lights installed at varying heights, depending upon whether they're being used for task or general room lighting, and to incorporate pendant styles rather than just traditional track heads.

Lighting Types

Just as your body wouldn't function well on a diet of just chicken or chickpeas, your kitchen won't function well with just one type of lighting. It requires a healthy diet of task and general lighting, with some optional accent lighting as dessert. Here are the major lighting types to consider when planning your space.

GENERAL/AMBIENT ROOM LIGHT

- This falls into two categories—natural sunlight and manufactured light designed to illuminate the overall space.

- Whenever possible, maximize natural sunlight for comfort, health, and enjoyment.

- Most manufactured general light sources are recessed ceiling cans or track, cable, or monorail lights if recessing isn't possible or desired.

- Chandeliers also are increasingly popular for ambient kitchen lighting.

TASK LIGHTING

- Task lighting is designed to focus targeted illumination where you're performing common kitchen tasks, like at the sink, cooktop, and countertop workspaces.

- It can be installed in the ceiling, like a recessed can above your kitchen sink, or under the wall cabinets directly above your work areas.

- Task lighting is also valuable at locations where kitchen occupants will read, do homework, eat, or play.

- These visible task lights are typically decorative fixtures like pendants above eat-at bars or small chandeliers above eat-in kitchen tables.

- Task lighting might also be installed within cabinets themselves, typically to illuminate dark corners or drawers when cabinets are opened.

above · Puck lights above the sink provide task lighting for meal prep and clean-up chores.

facing page top · Multiple windows and recessed can lights provide this kitchen's ambient room light.

ACCENT LIGHTING

- Some formal kitchens employ accent lighting to add drama to their space, which can include in-cabinet illumination to highlight a collection.

- Accent lights in a cabinet toekick or crown rope lighting on top of cabinets provides soft illumination to the space.

- Hiding accent lighting in architectural elements can help to emphasize those features, like the molding around a tray ceiling.

A variety of lighting types—
from undercabinet task lighting
to ambient lighting from multiple
ceiling fixtures—provides the
right amount of illumination.

The New LEDs

You've probably seen the LED acronym around your neighborhood electronics store or home center and wondered about the features and benefits of these relatively costly products. First, LED stands for *light-emitting diode*, tech-speak for a conducting element that gives off light (rather than current or data). Just as Edison's light bulb was a technological leap beyond the candle, an LED is a technological leap beyond the light bulb. LED is commonly used to describe both the technology itself, as in LED bulbs, or to describe fixtures, as in, "The electrician installed LEDs under the wall cabinets."

LED technology is available in different formats to serve all of your kitchen lighting needs:

- Most recently, standard bulb configurations that can replace halogens in your recessed ceiling lights or incandescents in your pendants or chandeliers.

- Task-lighting fixtures, including thin linear bars and compact pucks, that can light cabinet interiors or attach to their bottoms for lighting your countertops.

- Accent lighting in the form of flexible ropes that can tuck behind moldings to illuminate ceilings or face frames to showcase collectibles.

- Decorative lighting fixtures, like wall sconces, pendants, and track-light heads.

LED technology is significantly more energy efficient than both incandescent and compact fluorescent and can last for 10 to 20 years. This is a decided advantage for general room lighting—especially in larger kitchens with high ceilings, where changing out bulbs involves a ladder. With higher-wattage incandescents being phased out, long-lasting, energy-efficient, dimmable LEDs provide an excellent substitute.

above • LED task lights mounted to the bottom of wall cabinets make your countertop work areas brighter without heating up your hard-working hands.

right • New, in-drawer task lighting is well served by LED's stay-cool operation.

above • **LED technology adds energy efficiency and a longer bulb life to decorative pendants.**

above • **Versatile LED strips can be installed behind moldings, toekick valances, or within cabinets for accent lighting.**

LEDs don't heat up the way halogen or standard incandescent lights do. This makes them ideal for under-cabinet task lighting. Their cool operation also makes them ideal for in-cabinet applications, where an incandescent's heat might damage the cabinet or its contents over a long period of time.

More recently, LEDs have become available in a wide range of colors. They can also be specified as color-changing fixtures. These are perfect for places where accent lighting—and soft drama—is desired.

above • **Energy-efficient LED task lights make finding the contents of deep cabinets easier.**

Lighting

Lighting is essential to kitchens, and the best approach to getting all that you need is by layering it. This strategy of combining different types of lighting for different needs ensures that the room will be comfortable, attractive, and functional. Recessed, track, cable, or monorail lights can provide general room lighting. Pendants, undercabinet lights, and interior cabinet fixtures can provide crucial task lighting. Accent lighting is the icing on the lighting cake. It can be hidden behind moldings to accent decorative ceilings, inside built-ins to showcase collectibles, or even in a toekick to cast a soft nightlight glow in a room.

1. Pendants add both decorative style and essential task lighting to work and seating spaces. 2. Under-cabinet lighting illuminates countertop task areas and adds a feeling of spaciousness to your kitchen. 3. Chandeliers are now being used to add sparkle to a kitchen, just as they traditionally have for dining rooms and foyers. 4. Light fixtures with fabric work best at a safe distance from cooking surfaces where their shades could be splattered. 5. Accent lighting inside cabinets adds a soft glow to the room and the cabinet contents.

Paint and Other Wall Treatments

Kitchen paint has to be as durable and easy maintenance as possible. You want a finish that's scrubbable so you can get rid of food splatters and fingerprints without damaging the color. This typically means semi-gloss or satin, depending upon the brand you select.

When you start thinking about paint color, look for one that will enhance your cabinet finish, flooring, and countertop surfaces. These will be your largest visual surfaces, and they all need to coordinate with each other.

In general, cool tones like pale blues and sage greens work well with warm cabinet finishes like cherry and slate-style floors. Warm paints in the red and orange family work well with pale blonde maple cabinets and birch floors. Black and white countertop and cabinet surfaces give you numerous options to choose from; decide whether you want the room to have a warm or cool flavor, and choose colors from either side of the color wheel to enhance it.

All of your paint choices should be considered with the surrounding rooms in mind, too. One of the challenges many open-floor-plan kitchens present is where to start and stop room colors. Often, there's a doorway to mark the transition. If there isn't a bump-out or other natural marker, you might want to consider painting the conjoined rooms the same color for the best effect.

Some kitchens feature wall coverings other than paint. Wallpaper is one traditional choice. This selection can add pattern, as well as color, to your room. Just as with paint, it's important to choose a style in keeping

top · A paint color should coordinate with the elements of the kitchen and speak to your personal style as well.

right · Beadboard is an excellent, DIY-friendly way to enhance a focal-point wall.

with your other kitchen finishes. A heavily patterned wallpaper could be too busy with a heavily patterned countertop. Keep balance and scale in mind, just as you do when pairing countertops with cabinets and flooring. It's also important to consider local building codes and manufacturer specifications for wallpaper behind a cooking surface.

Tile, beadboard, wood paneling or wainscot, and tin (or faux tin) tiles are all alternatives to paint and wallpaper. Each of these can add color or texture to your kitchen as well as a unique decorative touch. Beadboard, paneling, and tin wall coverings work best in traditional spaces, whereas tile is versatile enough to work in any setting. Most kitchens don't cover all of their wall space with these materials; a little bit can go a long way. Be mindful of safety if installing wood products at a cooktop.

top left · **Don't forget your kitchen's fifth wall—its ceiling—when planning colors and coverings.**

left · **New paint is one of the easiest, most affordable ways to update a kitchen.**

Window and Door Coverings

Kitchen windows and doors present unique coverage challenges. Because they're highly likely to be exposed to grease, food, moisture, and fingerprints, any materials you choose should be easy to clean. Sliding and French doors that lead to the outside, as well as entry doors, get a tremendous amount of use, so be extra mindful of durability when choosing their coverings. Delicate or dry-clean-only fabrics aren't ideal for kitchen coverings.

Privacy is a concern for kitchens but not to the extent that it is for bathrooms or bedrooms, so a woven, cotton, or cellular shade that may reveal shadows from the outside can work fine in this space. Complete light control generally isn't an issue for a kitchen either, unless it opens to a home theater space, so natural woven shades made from bamboo, reeds, or matchsticks can also be considered.

Shutters and 2-inch wood or faux-wood blinds are excellent window covering choices. Coordinating styles are available for your kitchen doors—even the sliding patio variety. Draperies, café curtains, and valances are all potential options for a more traditional kitchen. Regardless of what kind of material you choose, keep fabric treatments away from your cooking surface.

above • Roman shades are popular window coverings for traditional kitchens, as they provide classic style, privacy, and flexible sunlight options.

above • Blinds are ideal window coverings for low maintenance, privacy, and light control. Faux-wood versions work best in very wet areas.

left • Woven shades are an excellent choice for privacy and light filtration in transitional kitchens.

below • Café curtains frequently dress up breakfast nooks, as they provide privacy to a seated diner while allowing ample light into the space.

Seating

Kitchen seating runs the gamut from built-in banquets to portable bar stools. Your kitchen configuration will influence many of your choices. If you have a narrow walkway behind your breakfast bar, a stool without a back that tucks easily under the countertop could be your best choice. If, on the other hand, you regularly entertain guests at your spacious island, comfortable bar or counter stools with arms and backs are a welcome choice.

If you're blessed with both counter seating and a table in your kitchen, you'll be able to find numerous suites of matching dining chairs and stools. Raised bars call for 30-inch bar stools. Standard kitchen countertop overhangs call for 24-inch counter stools. If your kitchen opens to your dining or family room, select finishes and fabrics that coordinate with other visible seating to create a cohesive open-plan space.

Banquettes or window seats are best upholstered in treated, outdoor-rated fabrics that will stand up to the food and drink spills that might hit them—especially in a busy family kitchen. These fabrics also work very well for stool cushions.

top right • Bar stools come in a range of styles and sizes. When they are lightweight or on casters, they're easy to more around for seating wherever it's needed.

right • Window seats can add storage and a comfortable perch for kitchen relaxation or socializing.

top · Banquettes are ideal for casual kitchen seating and are especially good for kids. Consider treated fabrics on cushions for easier cleanability.

above · Stools with backs and cushions provide greater comfort for entertaining and extended dining.

left · Counter stools provide seating at island or peninsula overhangs. Backless models that can be tucked underneath work best where there is limited space.

Personalizing Your Kitchen

One of the joys of creating a new kitchen is personalizing it with your own touches. There are numerous ways to do this—both big and small—depending on how long you plan to remain in the home and how much you want to invest.

Custom carvings and backsplash murals are two major ways to personalize a kitchen and need to be factored into your design process when you're working on cabinetry selections, tile, and lighting plans. Both can honor a family member, pet, vacation home, or other inspiration. Both will likely remain with the home when you move and should appeal to future owners if this isn't your "forever home."

On a smaller scale, you can choose cabinet hardware that speaks to a personal interest like gardening or countertop appliances with a retro feel to evoke your grandmother's kitchen.

Displaying artwork or collections is a popular way to personalize your space. Specially designed and illuminated built-ins or a spare wall can be used for this purpose. Just be sure that your valuables are suited to a kitchen's sometimes steamy, food-splattered environment and that they're out of harm's way in a busy space like this.

top right • Illuminated kitchen built-ins showcase a homeowner's collection while keeping it out of the work flow.

right • Plants can add a natural, health-enhancing note to your kitchen, while their carefully chosen pots contribute coordinated style.

Artwork personalizes a kitchen for both serious and casual collectors.

Updating and Personalizing an Existing Kitchen

So many kitchens today are generic rooms that reflect builder trends, not the homeowners who use them. Given how much time you spend in your kitchen, it's important to add personal elements that resonate with both your interests and existing design scheme (this is even more true if your kitchen is open to other spaces in your home).

Before you start decorating your kitchen, though, consider the shapes, finishes, styles, and textures already in the room and in adjacent open spaces. If your great room light fixtures are oil-rubbed bronze, for example, consider that finish for your kitchen lighting as well. If the appliances have stainless handles, consider coordinating brushed-nickel light fixtures. If you're adding crown molding to your kitchen—on its cabinets, ceiling, or both—choose a style that coordinates with the moldings and casings in adjacent rooms. This will unify the home's architecture in an appealing manner.

Beyond fixtures, trim, and window treatments, think about color scheme. Even if your kitchen is not open to adjacent rooms, the transition into and out of the kitchen shouldn't be jarring. Select coordinating colors so that rooms better tie together visually.

A fresh coat of soft blue paint complements the flooring, trusses, and cabinetry while providing a handsome backdrop for the homeowner's artwork.

A small storage cabinet creates a compact landing zone for keys, bags, and mail next to the doorway. Its smooth white finish coordinates with the white kitchen countertops.

A new outdoor-rated rug adds freshness (and cleanability) to the space and pulls its colors from the paint, artwork, baskets, and cabinetry.

THE EXISTING ROOM

Light, color, fabric, and storage can update a dark, heavy kitchen with new style and functionality.

Sleeker track lighting can offer updated style and energy-efficient, durable LED technology to this kitchen.

A Made-to-Order Kitchen

A homey kitchen full of art and memories was at the top of the homeowner's wish list when she built her Long Island, New York, home. It was designed to be a gathering room where she could surround herself with her favorite pieces and people. Multiple sets of open shelves as well as glass-front cabinets all facilitate her desire to display.

With artwork and decorative elements adding color and pattern, the quiet hues surrounding the white cabinets and muted countertops keep the kitchen from feeling cluttered or busy. Instead, they enhance the feeling of being in a beachside gallery rather than a residential kitchen. The bare chandelier coordinates with simple door and window coverings that heighten the unadorned impression and further draw your eye back to the artwork.

above • Open shelves hold collectibles and flowers in the cooking zone, personalizing it for an art-loving homeowner.

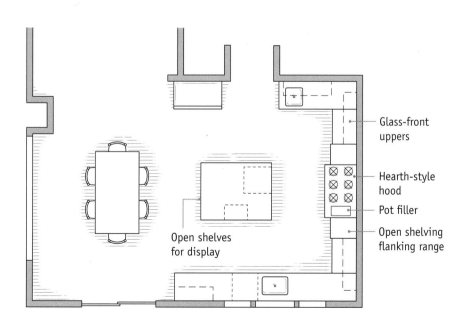

Open shelves for display

Glass-front uppers

Hearth-style hood

Pot filler

Open shelving flanking range

left • Surprising details, like the finish of the black-and-mirrored sconce, keep the space from being overly formal or cliché.

above • While embracing professional-caliber appliances and fixtures suitable for serious home entertaining, this kitchen was designed to be an art-filled space for comfortable, casual socializing.

CREDITS

p. i: © Mark Lohman

p. ii: © Randy O'Rourke, architect: Frank Shirley

p. iv (left to right): © Mark Lohman, design: RaeLynn Callaway; © Randy O'Rourke, design: Kent Kitchen Works; Tresco Lighting by Rev-A Shelf, LLC; © Randy O'Rourke, design: Jake Wright, Turkel Design, turkeldesign.com, 518-695-3560; © Greg Riegler, design: Cheryl Kees Clendenon, InDetail Interiors

p. v (left to right): © Susan Teare, architect: Hart Associates Architects, Inc., interior design: SLC Interiors, builder: Sea-Dar Construction; © Ryann Ford, design: Clayton Morgan Design Consultant; © Susan Teare, architect: Elizabeth Herrmann, AIA, Elizabeth Herrmann Architecture + Design, Bristol, VT, builder: Northern Timbers Construction, cabinets: Ben Lucarelli Woodworks; © Tria Giovan, design: Cathy Chapman; © Greg Riegler, design: Cheryl Kees Clendenon, InDetail Interiors

p. vii: © Mark Lohman, design: Cynthia Marks Design

p. 1: © Susan Teare, design: Michael Minadeo + Partners

p. 2 (top, left to right): provided by Formica Corporation; Craft Art Elegant Surfaces, www.craft-art.com; © Mark Lohman, design: Cynthia Marks Interior Design; © Tria Giovan, design: Sandoval Blanda Architects and Interiors; design: Jamie Gold, Jamie Gold Kitchen and Bath Design, LLC, www.jgkitchens.com, with Terry Smith Cabinetry and Design, www.terrysmithdesign.com; (bottom): © Ryann Ford, design: The Renner Project, www.therennerproject.com

CHAPTER 1

p. 4: © Tria Giovan, design: John Bjornen

p. 6: © Ryann Ford, design: Sara Scaglione, Shabby Slips, www.shabbyslipsaustin.com

p. 7 (top): © Susan Teare, architect: Elizabeth Herrmann, AIA, Elizabeth Herrmann Architecture + Design, Bristol, VT; (bottom): © Susan Teare, architect: Hart Associates Architects, Inc., builder: Kistler and Knapp Builders

p. 8 (top): © Tria Giovan; (bottom): © Mark Lohman

p. 9: © Ryann Ford, interior design: Jerri Kunz, www.jerrikunz.com

p. 10-11: © Tria Giovan

p. 11 (right): © Susan Teare, architect: Ernest Ruskey, AIA, Tektonika Studio Architects, Stowe, VT, 802-253-2020, www.tektonikavt.com, builder: Peregrine Design Build

p. 12-13: © William Geddes, design: Krieger Architects

p. 14 (top right): courtesy Smith+Noble, www.smithandnoble.com; (bottom right): KraftMaid Cabinetry

p. 15 (large): Roe Osborn, courtesy *Fine Homebuilding* magazine, © The Taunton Press, Inc.; (small): Cambrian Black, courtesy of Cambria®

p. 16 (top): © Mark Lohman; (bottom): © Susan Teare, architect: Birdseye Design, builder: Alec Genung Construction Inc.

p. 17: © Susan Teare, design: Michael Minadeo + Partners

p. 18 (bottom): © Ryann Ford, design: Miro Rivera Architects, www.mirorivera.com, builder: Don Crowell Inc.

p. 18-19: © Randy O'Rourke, design: Henry Chalmers, Old World Design & Construction

p. 19 (bottom right): © Susan Teare, architect: Ernest Ruskey, AIA, Tektonika Studio Architects, Stowe, Vermont, 802-253-2020, www.tektonikavt.com, builder: Gristmill Builders

p. 20-21: design: Douglah Designs

p. 21 (right): design: Douglah Designs

p. 22: courtesy Zephyr

p. 23 (top): photograph supplied by TORLYS Smart Floors, www.torlys.com; (bottom left): © William Geddes, design: Krieger Architects; (bottom right): courtesy Quality Cabinets

p. 24-25: © Ken Gutmaker, design: McElroy Architecture

p. 27: © Ryann Ford, design: ARB Homes & Design, www.arbhomes.com, interior design: Jennifer Tuthill-Johnson Décor; (bottom): © Susan Teare, design: Michael Minadeo + Partners

p. 28-29: © Susan Teare, builder: Peregrine Design Build

p. 28: © Susan Teare, architect: Elizabeth Herrmann, AIA, Elizabeth Herrmann Architecture + Design, Bristol, VT, builder: Northern Timbers Construction

p. 29 (bottom): © Susan Teare, design: Hatch + Ulland Owen Architects, www.huoarchitects.com

CHAPTER 2

p. 30: © Tria Giovan, design: Sandoval Blanda Architects and Interiors

p. 32 (top): © Susan Teare, design: Joan Heaton Architects, builder: Silver Maple Construction, cabinets: Ober Woodworking; (bottom): © Ryann Ford, design: Kelly Moseley, www.anabelinteriors.com

p. 33: © Tria Giovan, design: Marshall Watson

p. 34: © Susan Teare, kitchen design: Cushman Design Group, project designer: Milford Cushman, lighting over counter: Arroyo Craftsman, lighting over table: Hubbardton Forge

p. 35 (top): © Ryann Ford, architect: Frank Welch & Associates, www.frankwelch.com; (bottom): © Susan Teare, builder: Peregrine Design Build

p. 36-37: © Chris Giles, design: Lisa Wilson-Wirth, CKD, Wilson-Wirth Design, www.wilsonwirthdesign.com

p. 38: courtesy BLANCO, www.blancoamerica.com

p. 39 (top left): © William Geddes, design: Thomas Richard, TRS Designs, Inc., cabinetry and appliances: Robert McCaughern, general contractor; (top right): The Entertainer Sink by Lenova, www.lenovasinks.com; (bottom left): courtesy Quality Cabinets; (bottom right): courtesy KitchenAid®

p. 40 (top): © Susan Teare, designer/builder: Classic Home, Charlotte, VT; (bottom): © Susan Teare, contractor: Reap Construction, Ltd., Richmond, VT, design: Jenny Volk, Signature Kitchens at Rice Lumber, Shelburne, VT

p. 41 (top): © Tria Giovan, design: Bellacasa Design; (bottom): © Ryann Ford, interior design: Suzie Page, Twenty Three 07, www.twentythree07.com

p. 42-43: © William Geddes, design: Thomas Richard, TRS Designs, Inc., cabinetry and appliances: Robert McCaughern, general contractor

p. 44-45: © Susan Teare, contractor: Reap Construction, Ltd., Richmond, VT, design: Jenny Volk, Signature Kitchens at Rice Lumber, Shelburne, VT

p. 44 (bottom): courtesy Minimal USA

p. 45 (bottom): © Susan Teare, architect: Elizabeth Herrmann, AIA, Elizabeth Herrmann Architecture + Design, Bristol, VT

p. 46-47 (large): Scott Phillips, © The Taunton Press, Inc.

p. 46 (top left): courtesy LG; (bottom): Rev-A-Shelf, LLC

p. 47 (top): courtesy IKEA®; (bottom): Staron® Solid Surfaces

p. 48-49: design: Jamie Gold, Jamie Gold Kitchen and Bath Design, LLC, www.jgkitchens.com, with Terry Smith Cabinetry and Design, www.terrysmithdesign.com

CHAPTER 3

p. 50: © Tria Giovan, design: Cathy Chapman

p. 52 (top): design: Jamie Gold, Jamie Gold Kitchen and Bath Design, LLC, www.jgkitchens.com, with Terry Smith Cabinetry and Design, www.terrysmithdesign.com; (bottom): © Susan Teare, builder: Reap Construction, Ltd., Richmond, VT, design: Joy Reap, Heike Doane and Simpson Cabinetry, custom cabinets: Simpson Cabinetry, South Burlington, VT

p. 53 (top): © Susan Teare, architect: Elizabeth Herrmann, AIA, Elizabeth Herrmann Architecture + Design, Bristol, VT; (bottom): © Susan Teare, builder: Peregrine Design Build

p. 54: (top): © Susan Teare, architect/interior designer: Mitra Samimi-Urich, Mitra Designs Studio for Architecture and Interiors, Bristol, VT; (bottom): © Susan Teare, architect: Brad Rabinowitz Architect, Burlington, VT, www.bradrabinowitzarchitect.com

p. 55: © Mark Lohman, design: EBTA Architects

p. 56 (top): design: Jamie Gold, Jamie Gold Kitchen and Bath Design, LLC, www.jgkitchens.com, with Terry Smith Cabinetry and Design, www.terrysmithdesign.com; (bottom): © William Geddes, design: Krieger Architects

p. 57 (left): © Susan Teare, designer/builder: Classic Home, Charlotte, VT; (right): © Susan Teare, design: Joan Heaton Architects, builder: Silver Maple Construction, cabinets: Ober Woodworking

p. 58 (top): © 2012 Showplace Cabinetry, www.ShowplaceWood.com; (bottom): Atlas Homewares

p. 59 (large): Brian Pontolilo, courtesy *Fine Homebuilding* magazine, © The Taunton Press, Inc.; (bottom left): Atlas Homewares; (bottom right): Rev-A-Shelf, LLC

p. 60 (top): Breathe Easy® Cabinetry; (bottom): Breathe Easy® Cabinetry, courtesy Jeaninne M. Comstock, interior designer, JMC Interiors, JMCInteriorDesigns.com

p. 61 (top and bottom): courtesy Bornholm Kitchen, www.bornholmkitchen.com

p. 62: © Ken Gutmaker, design: Kelly and Carol Morisseau, www.mainstreetkitchens.com

p. 63 (top left): © William Geddes, design: Thomas Richard, TRS Designs, Inc., cabinetry and appliances: Robert McCaughern, general contractor; (top right): © William Geddes, design: Tara Andersen, Park Slope Kitchen Gallery, www.parkslopekitchengallery.com; (bottom): courtesy Quality Cabinets

p. 64 (top): courtesy Quality Cabinets; (bottom): Courtesy KraftMaid Cabinetry

p. 65 (top): Courtesy Kitchen Craft Cabinetry; (bottom): courtesy Quality Cabinets

p. 66 (top): courtesy IKEA®; (bottom): design: Kuche+Cucina (www.kuche-cucina.com); product: Pedini (www.pediniusa.com)

p. 67: Poggenpohl

p. 68-69: © Jo-Ann Richards, design: The Sky is the Limit Design

p. 70 (top): © Ken Gutmaker, design: Kelly and Carol Morisseau, www.mainstreetkitchens.com; (bottom): Mark Lohman

p. 71 (top left and bottom right): © Randy O'Rourke, design: Kent Kitchen Works; (bottom left): © William Geddes, design: Thomas Richard, TRS Designs, Inc., cabinetry and appliances: Robert McCaughern, general contractor

p. 72 (top and bottom): Rev-A-Shelf, LLC

p. 73 (top): Rev-A-Shelf, LLC; (bottom): © Ken Gutmaker, design: Kelly and Carol Morisseau, www.mainstreetkitchens.com

p. 74 (top): © Jo-Ann Richards, design: The Sky is the Limit Design; (bottom): © Ken Gutmaker, design: McElroy Architecture

p. 75 (top): © Jo-Ann Richards, design: The Sky is the Limit Design; (bottom): © William Geddes, design: Krieger Architects

p. 76 (top): © William Geddes, design: Krieger Architects; (bottom): © Greg Riegler, design: Cheryl Kees Clendenon, InDetail Interiors

p. 77 (top left): © Ken Gutmaker, design: McElroy Architecture; (bottom left): © Greg Riegler, design: Cheryl Kees Clendenon, InDetail Interiors; (right): © William Geddes, design: Krieger Architects

p. 78-79: © Greg Riegler, design: Cheryl Kees Clendenon, InDetail Interiors

CHAPTER 4

p. 80: © Susan Teare, builder: Peregrine Design Build

p. 82: © Susan Teare, interior design: Des-Syn of Atlanta, GA, location: South Village, South Burlington, VT

p. 83 (top): © William Geddes, design: Thomas Richard, TRS Designs, Inc., cabinetry and appliances: Robert McCaughern, general contractor; (bottom left): © Jo-Ann Richards, design: The Sky is the Limit Design; (bottom right): © Chris Giles, design: Lisa Wilson-Wirth, CKD, Wilson-Wirth Design, www.wilsonwirthdesign.com

p. 84 (top left and bottom left): Electrolux Appliances, www.electroluxappliances.com

p. 85 (large): David Ericson, courtesy *Fine Homebuilding* magazine; (top right and bottom right): Electrolux Appliances, www.electroluxappliances.com

p. 86: © Randy O'Rourke, design: Shelly Cryer using IKEA®

p. 87 (top): © Randy O'Rourke, design: Kent Kitchen Works; (bottom left): © Susan Teare, builder: Peregrine Design Build; (bottom right): © Mark Lohman

p. 88: © Susan Teare, architect: Hart Associates Architects, Inc., builder: Kistler and Knapp Builders; (bottom): © Ken Gutmaker, design: Kelly and Carol Morisseau, www.mainstreetkitchens.com

p. 89: © Greg Riegler, design: Cheryl Kees Clendenon, InDetail Interiors

p. 90 (top): © Chris Giles, design: Lisa Wilson-Wirth, CKD, Wilson-Wirth Design, www.wilsonwirthdesign.com; (bottom): © Ken Gutmaker, design: McElroy Architecture

p. 91: © Mark Lohman

p. 92 (top): © Mark Lohman; (bottom): © William Geddes, design: Thomas Richard, TRS Designs, Inc., cabinetry and appliances: Robert McCaughern, general contractor

p. 93 (left): © Mark Lohman, design: Michael Lee Architect; (top right): Vent-A-Hood NPH9 Under Cabinet Hood; (bottom right): © Susan Teare, kitchen, cabinetry, and finishes designed by Cushman Design Group, project designer: Chad Forcier, general contractor: Gristmill Builders, cabinetry: Gristmill Builders, countertops: Soapstone and Hardwood, range: Wolf

p. 94-95: © Tria Giovan

p. 95 (top and bottom right): © William Geddes, design: Thomas Richard, TRS Designs, Inc., cabinetry and appliances: Robert McCaughern, general contractor

p. 96 (top): © Greg Riegler, design: Cheryl Kees Clendenon, InDetail Interiors; (bottom): © Jo-Ann Richards, design: The Sky is the Limit Design

p. 97 (left): © Greg Riegler, design: Cheryl Kees Clendenon, InDetail Interiors; (right): © Ken Gutmaker, design: Kahn Design Associates, designer: Tiffany Leichter, www.kda-berkeley.com

p. 98 (top): © William Geddes, design: Tara Andersen, Park Slope Kitchen Gallery, www.parkslopekitchengallery.com

p. 99 (top left): © Greg Riegler, design: Cheryl Kees Clendenon, InDetail Interiors; (top right): © Susan Teare, design: Studio III Architects, Bristol, VT, www.Studio3architects.net, general contractor: Silver Maple Construction, cabinet fabricators: Stark Mountain Wood Working, Kitchen design and metal work design: Studio III, blacksmith fabrication work: Huntington River Smithy; (bottom): courtesy Thermador

p. 100 (top): © Tria Giovan; (bottom): © William Geddes, design: Thomas Richard, TRS Designs, Inc., cabinetry and appliances: Robert McCaughern, general contractor

p. 101: © Susan Teare, design: Cushman Design Group, inc.

p. 102 (top): © Tria Giovan; (bottom): © Greg Riegler, design: Cheryl Kees Clendenon, InDetail Interiors

p. 103 (left): courtesy KitchenAid®; (right): © Greg Riegler, design: Cheryl Kees Clendenon, InDetail Interiors

p. 104 (top): © GE Appliances 2012; (bottom): Sharp Electronics Corporation

p. 105 (top): Fisher & Paykel Appliances, Inc.; (bottom left): © GE Appliances 2012; (bottom right): courtesy Thermador

p. 106 (top): © Mark Lohman, architect: Quentin Dart Parker; (bottom): © Susan Teare, design: North Woods Joinery, www.nwjoinery.com

p. 107 (top): © Mark Lohman; design: Janet Lohman Interior Design; (bottom left): © Randy O'Rourke, design: Kent Kitchen Works; (bottom right): Innovative Product Sales Intl

p. 108-109: © Greg Riegler, design: Cheryl Kees Clendenon, InDetail Interiors

CHAPTER 5

p. 110: © Susan Teare, architect: Hart Associates Architects, Inc., interior design: SLC Interiors, builder: Sea-Dar Construction

p. 112 (top): © William Geddes, design: Krieger Architects; (bottom): © Ken Gutmaker, design: McElroy Architecture

p. 113: design: Jamie Gold, Jamie Gold Kitchen and Bath Design, LLC, www.jgkitchens.com, with Terry Smith Cabinetry and Design, www.terrysmithdesign.com

p. 114: © Ken Gutmaker, design: Kahn Design Associates, designer: Tiffany Leichter, www.kda-berkeley.com

p. 115 (left): © Greg Riegler, design: Cheryl Kees Clendenon, InDetail Interiors; (right): © Ken Gutmaker, design: McElroy Architecture

p. 116 (top): © William Geddes, design: Tara Andersen, Park Slope Kitchen Gallery, www.parkslopekitchengallery.com; (bottom): © Greg Riegler, design: Cheryl Kees Clendenon, InDetail Interiors

p. 117 (top): © Randy O'Rourke, design: Colangelo Associates Architects (colangeloassociates.com); (bottom left): © William Geddes, design: Tara Andersen, Park Slope Kitchen Gallery, www.parkslopekitchengallery.com; (bottom right): © Ken Gutmaker, design: McElroy Architecture

p. 118 (top): Formica Corporation; (bottom): courtesy Sonoma Cast Stone

p. 119: Formica Corporation

p. 120 (top): Craft Art Elegant Surfaces, www.craft-art.com; (bottom left): © Ken Gutmaker, design: Kahn Design Associates, designer: Tiffany Leichter, www.kda-berkeley.com; (bottom right): © Greg Riegler, design: Cheryl Kees Clendenon, InDetail Interiors

p. 121: Craft Art Elegant Surfaces, www.craft-art.com

p. 122-123: © William Geddes, design: Tara Andersen, Park Slope Kitchen Gallery, www.parkslopekitchengallery.com

p. 124 (top and bottom): Formica Corporation

p. 125 (top): © Ryann Ford, design: Clayton Morgan Design Consultant; (bottom left): © Susan Teare, builder: Peregrine Design Build; (bottom right): © Ken Gutmaker, design: Kahn Design Associates, designer: Tiffany Leichter, www.kda-berkeley.com

p. 126: Staron® Solid Surfaces

p. 127: (left): Roe Osborn, courtesy *Fine Homebuilding* magazine, © The Taunton Press, Inc.; (top right): Kensington Courtesy of Cambria®; (bottom right): Seipp Wohnen, Waldshut-Tiengen, Germany

p. 128-129: courtesy The Size—a Tile of Spain branded manufacturer, www.tileofspainusa.com

p. 129 (top): Seipp Wohnen, Waldshut-Tiengen, Germany; (bottom): courtesy The Size—a Tile of Spain branded manufacturer, www.tileofspainusa.com

p. 130-131: Jamie Gold, Jamie Gold Kitchen and Bath Design, LLC, www.jgkitchens.com, with Terry Smith Cabinetry and Design, terrysmithdesign.com

p. 130 (bottom): © Jo-Ann Richards, design: The Sky is the Limit Design

p. 131 (bottom): © Tria Giovan

p. 132 (top): © Ken Gutmaker, design: Kahn Design Associates, designer: Tiffany Leichter, www.kda-berkeley.com; (bottom): © Greg Riegler, design: Cheryl Kees Clendenon, InDetail Interiors

p. 133 (top): design: Jennifer Ho, CKD, CBD, CID; (bottom): design: InDetail Interiors

p. 134-135: © Tria Giovan, design: Brady Design

p. 134 (bottom): courtesy Crossville, Inc., www.crossvilleinc.com

p. 135 (top right): © William Geddes, design: Thomas Richard, TRS Designs, Inc., cabinetry and appliances: Robert McCaughern, general contractor; (bottom left): © Mark Lohman; (bottom right): © Mark Lohman, design: ROHL

p. 136: © Randy O'Rourke, design: Kent Kitchen Works

p. 137 (top left): courtesy IKEA®; (bottom left): © Mark Lohman, design: Janet Lohman Interior Design; (right): © Mark Lohman

CREDITS

p. 138-139: © Ken Gutmaker, architect: Robert Wylie Architects, interior design: Suzanne Miller, tile design: Laura Myers, Bella Tile Design, teacup mosaic: Karen Thompson, Archetile Mosaics

CHAPTER 6

p. 140: © Ryann Ford, design/build: The Renner Project, www.therennerproject.com

p. 142: © Susan Teare, design: Hart Associates Architects, Inc., SLC Interiors, Sea-Dar Construction

p. 143 (top): Greg Riegler, design: Cheryl Kees Clendenon, InDetail Interiors; (bottom left and bottom right): © Mark Lohman, design: Barclay Butera Inc.

p. 144-145 (top): © Susan Teare, designed and built by Conner & Buck Builders; (bottom): © Randy O'Rourke, architect: Frank Shirley

p. 145: © Susan Teare, architect: Jean Terwilliger

p. 146 (top): courtesy Forbo Flooring Systems; (center): courtesy Forbo Flooring Systems; (bottom): courtesy Tarkett, Inc.

p. 147 (left): © Mark Lohman; (top right): Crossville, Inc., www.crossvilleinc.com; (bottom right): photograph supplied by TORLYS Smart Floors, www.torlys.com

p. 148: © Susan Teare, design: Michael Minadeo + Partners

p. 149 (top): © Susan Teare, architect: Elizabeth Herrmann, AIA, Elizabeth Herrmann Architecture + Design, Bristol, VT, builder: Northern Timbers Construction, cabinets: Ben Lucarelli Woodworks; (bottom): © Susan Teare, interior design: Pam Carter, Keeping Good Company in Addison, VT, South Burlington, VT

p. 150 (left): © Susan Teare, architect: Brad Rabinowitz Architect, Burlington, VT, 802-658-0430, www.bradrabinowitzarchitect.com; (right): © Ken Gutmaker, design: Kahn Design Associates, designer: Tiffany Leichter, www.kda-berkeley.com

p. 151 (top): © Susan Teare, builder: Peregrine Design Build; (bottom): © William Geddes, design: Krieger Architects

p. 152 (top): © Susan Teare, builder: Peregrine Design Build; (bottom): © Susan Teare, kitchen, cabinetry, and finishes designed by Cushman Design Group, project designer: Kelley Osgood, cabinetry: Whit Hartt, counter: Granite–Kodiak Brown (honed)

p. 153: © Tria Giovan

p. 154 (top): © Susan Teare, Vermont Eco-Floors, Exposed Aggregate Finish; (bottom): © Chris Giles, design: Lisa Wilson-Wirth, CKD, Wilson-Wirth Design, www.wilsonwirthdesign.com

p. 155: © Susan Teare, design: Studio III Architects, Bristol, VT, www.Studio3architects.net, general contractor: Silver Maple Construction, cabinet fabricators: Stark Mountain Wood Working; Kitchen design and metal work design: Studio III, blacksmith fabrication work: Huntington River Smithy

p. 156: © Settecento

p. 157 (top): courtesy Apavisa—a Tile of Spain branded manufacturer, www.tileofspainusa.com; (bottom left): © Impronta; (bottom right): © Settecento

p. 158 (top): Baroque Sienna plank by WE Cork; (bottom): © Jo-Ann Richards, design: The Sky is the Limit Design

p. 160: © Ryann Ford, design: The Renner Project, www.therennerproject.com

p. 161 (left): courtesy Crossville, Inc., www.crossvilleinc.com; (right): © Mark Lohman, design: Janet Lohman Interior Design

p. 162-163: © Ken Gutmaker, design: Kelly and Carol Morisseau, www.mainstreetkitchens.com

CHAPTER 7

p. 164: © Mark Lohman

p. 166: © William Geddes, design: Thomas Richard, TRS Designs, Inc., cabinetry and appliances: Robert McCaughern, general contractor

p. 167 (left): © Susan Teare, architect: Elizabeth Herrmann, AIA, Elizabeth Herrmann Architecture + Design, Bristol, VT, builder: Northern Timbers Construction, cabinets: Ben Lucarelli Woodworks; (right): © Susan Teare, builder: Peregrine Design Build

p. 168: © Ken Gutmaker, design: Kelly and Carol Morisseau, www.mainstreetkitchens.com

p. 169: © Mark Lohman

p. 170: Elkay Avado Sink courtesy Elkay, visit www.elkayusa.com for more information

p. 171 (top left): Brian Potolilo, courtesy *Fine Homebuilding*, © The Taunton Press, Inc.; (top right): © Delta Faucet Company; (bottom left): courtesy BLANCO, www.blancoamerica.com; (bottom right): courtesy Karran Sinks

p. 172 (top): © Tria Giovan; (bottom): Greg Riegler, design: Cheryl Kees Clendenon, InDetail Interiors

p. 173 (left): © Susan Teare, design: kitchen, cabinetry, and finishes designed by Cushman Design Group, project designer: Kelley Osgood, cabinetry: Whit Hartt, counter: Granite–Kodiak Brown (honed); (right): © Greg Riegler, design: Cheryl Kees Clendenon, InDetail Interiors

p. 174-175: © Jo-Ann Richards, design: The Sky is the Limit Design

p. 176 (top): © Greg Riegler, design: Cheryl Kees Clendenon, InDetail Interiors; (bottom): © Ken Gutmaker, design: McElroy Architecture

p. 177: © Mark Lohman, design: Cynthia Marks Interior Design

p. 178 (top): © Susan Teare; (bottom): ROHL Perrin & Rowe 4-hole kitchen faucet with side spray in Inca Brass Finish, photographed in a Clive Christian showroom

p. 179 (top): © William Geddes, design: Krieger Architects; (bottom): © William Geddes, design: Thomas Richard, TRS Designs, Inc., cabinetry and appliances: Robert McCaughern, general contractor

p. 180 (top): © Delta Faucet Company; (bottom): © Delta Faucet Company

p. 181 (top left): © Delta Faucet Company; (top right and bottom): © Delta Faucet Company

p. 182 (top): © Mark Lohman, design: Michael Lee Architect; (bottom): © Greg Riegler, design: Cheryl Kees Clendenon, InDetail Interiors

p. 183 (top): © Greg Riegler, design: Cheryl Kees Clendenon, InDetail Interiors; (bottom left): courtesy Hansgrohe; (bottom right): InSinkErator®

CHAPTER 8

p. 184: © Mark Lohman

p. 186-187: © Susan Teare, architect: Ernest Ruskey, AIA, Tektonika Studio Architects, Stowe, VT, 802-253-2020, www.tektonikavt.com, builder: Peregrine Design Build

p. 186 (bottom): © Mark Lohman, design: Kristy Kropat Interior Design

p. 187 (bottom): © Mark Lohman, design: Cynthia Marks Design

p. 188-189: © Ken Gutmaker, design: Kahn Design Associates, designer: Tiffany Leichter, www.kda-berkeley.com

p. 190: © Mark Lohman, design: RaeLynn Callaway

p. 191 (top): © Susan Teare, kitchen design: Cushman Design Group, project designer: Milford Cushman, lighting over counter: Arroyo Craftsman, lighting over table: Hubbardton Forge; (bottom): © Jo-Ann Richards, Design: The Sky is the Limit Design

p. 192: © Mark Lohman

p. 193 (top): © Susan Teare, builder: Peregrine Design Build; (bottom): © Randy O'Rourke, design: Kent Kitchen Works

p. 194 (top): Tresco Lighting by Rev-A Shelf, LLC; (bottom): courtesy Rev-A-Shelf, LLC

p. 195 (top): Bruck Lighting Systems, Inc.; (bottom left): courtesy Rev-A-Shelf, LLC; (bottom right): courtesy Rev-A-Shelf, LLC

p. 196 (top): © Ken Gutmaker, design: McElroy Architecture; (bottom left): © William Geddes, design: Tara Andersen, Park Slope Kitchen Gallery, www.parkslopekitchengallery.com; (bottom right): © Susan Teare, design: Hart Associates Architects, Inc., SLC Interiors

p. 197 (left): © Ryann Ford, design: Jim Poteet, Poteet Architects, www.poteetarchitects.com; (right): © Susan Teare, kitchen, cabinetry, and finishes designed by Cushman Design Group, project designer: Chad Forcier, general contractor: Donald P. Blake Jr. Inc., cabinetry: Derek Barrett, species: cherry, finish: Sutherland Welles Polymerized Tung Oil, light fixtures: Brass Light Gallery

p. 198 (top): © Mark Lohman; (bottom): © Susan Teare, builder: Peregrine Design Build

p. 199 (top): © Susan Teare, design: Joan Heaton Architects, builder: Silver Maple Construction, cabinets: Ober Woodworking; (bottom): © Mark Lohman

p. 200 (top): © Tria Giovan, design: Cathy Chapman; (bottom): © Mark Lohman

p. 201 (top): © William Geddes, design: Tara Andersen, Park Slope Kitchen Gallery, www.parkslopekitchengallery.com; (bottom): © Greg Riegler, design: Cheryl Kees Clendenon, InDetail Interiors

p. 202 (top): © Tria Giovan; (bottom): © Mark Lohman

p. 203 (top): © Randy O'Rourke, design: Kent Kitchen Works; (bottom left): © Ken Gutmaker, design: McElroy Architecture; (bottom right): © Mark Lohman

p. 204 (top): © Ryann Ford, design: Barley & Pfeiffer Architects, www.barleypfeiffer.com; (bottom): © Ryann Ford, interior design: Suzie Page, Twenty Three 07, www.twentythree07.com

p. 205: © Susan Teare, architect: Brad Rabinowitz Architect, Burlington, VT, 802-658-0430, www.bradrabinowitzarchitect.com

p. 206 (top): Sherwin-Williams Atmospheric (SW6505); (center): Grandin Road, available at www.grandinroad.com; (bottom): Grandin Road, available at www.grandinroad.com

p. 207 (large): Brian Vanden Brink, courtesy *Fine Homebuilding* magazine; (bottom right): photograph provided by Kichler Lighting

p. 208-209: © William Geddes, design: Susan Serra, CKD, CAPS, Bornholm Kitchen, www.BornholmKitchen.com

INDEX

INDEX

If you like this book, you'll love *Fine Homebuilding*.

Read *Fine Homebuilding* Magazine:

Get eight issues, including our two annual design issues, *Houses and Kitchens & Baths*, plus FREE iPad digital access. Packed with expert advice and skill-building techniques, every issue provides the latest information on quality building and remodeling.

Subscribe today at:
FineHomebuilding.com/4Sub

Discover our *Fine Homebuilding* Online Store:

It's your destination for premium resources from America's best builders: how-to and design books, DVDs, videos, special interest publications, and more.

Visit today at:
FineHomebuilding.com/4More

Get our FREE *Fine Homebuilding* eNewsletter:

Keep up with the current best practices, the newest tools, and the latest materials, plus free tips and advice from *Fine Homebuilding* editors.

Sign up, it's free:
FineHomebuilding.com/4Newsletter

Become a FineHomebuilding.com member

Join to enjoy unlimited access to premium content and exclusive benefits, including: 1,400+ articles; 350 tip, tool, and technique videos; our how-to video project series; over 1,600 field-tested tips; monthly giveaways; digital issues; contests; special offers, and more.

Discover more information online:
FineHomebuilding.com/4Join